PRAYER OF PETITION

Jerry Savelle is a man that I've admired for years. He's filled with the wisdom and knowledge of God. He has lived his life openly and well and is an inspiration to many people, including me. I'm so excited for *Prayer of Petition* because I know that contained in the pages of this book are words that have the power to forever change people's lives.

JOHN BEVERE
Author and speaker, Messenger International
(www.messengerinternational.org)
Colorado Springs, Colorado/Australia/United Kingdom

I remember Mrs. Kenneth E. Hagin, Sr. (Oretha), tellling me, "Jerry Savelle is my favorite." (Of course, she excluded her husband, who was the apostle of faith to all of us.) That was quite a recommendation! Jerry has an ability to put forth the powerful principles of faith in an easily understandable way, showing how to apply them to one's own life.

BILLYE BRIM
Founder, Billye Brim Ministries (www.billyebrim.org)
Kirbyville, Missouri

I encourage you to read Jerry Savelle's book *Prayer of Petition*. Jerry and Carolyn Savelle have lived by supernatural faith for many years. Jerry's knowledge and wisdom are extremely valuable.

GLORIA COPELAND
Cofounder, Kenneth Copeland Ministries (www.kcm.org)
Fort Worth, Texas

I'm convinced that every failure in life is a prayer failure. Unfortunately, many believers fail in life because they simply don't know how to pray. *Prayer of Petition* is a power-packed prayer handbook for all Christians at any stage of the Christian walk. This book is a dynamic, timeless classic that should be in everyone's personal library. It will inspire readers to pray and believe for the impossible.

CREFLO DOLLAR
Founder and senior pastor, World Changers Church International
Founder, Creflo Dollar Ministries (www.creflodollarministries.org)
College Park, Georgia

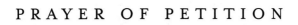

PRAYER OF PETITION

JERRY SAVELLE

PRAYER

—of—

PETITION

BREAKING THROUGH THE IMPOSSIBLE

Regal

From Gospel Light
Ventura, California, U.S.A.

Published by Regal
From Gospel Light
Ventura, California, U.S.A.
www.regalbooks.com
Printed in the U.S.A.

All Scripture quotations, unless otherwise indicated,
are taken from the Authorized King James Version.

Other versions used are
AMP—Scripture taken from THE AMPLIFIED BIBLE, Old Testament copyright © 1965,
1987 by the Zondervan Corporation. The Amplified New Testament copyright © 1958,
1987 by The Lockman Foundation. Used by permission.
ASV—The *American Standard Version,* Thomas Nelson and Sons, first published in 1901.
THE MESSAGE—Scripture taken from *THE MESSAGE.* Copyright © by Eugene H. Peterson,
1993, 1994, 1995. Used by permission of NavPress Publishing Group.
NASB—Scripture taken from the *New American Standard Bible,* © 1960, 1962, 1963, 1968,
1971, 1972, 1973, 1975, 1977, 1995 by The Lockman Foundation. Used by permission.
NIV—Scripture taken from the *Holy Bible, New International Version*®. Copyright © 1973,
1978, 1984 by International Bible Society. Used by permission of Zondervan
Publishing House. All rights reserved.
NKJV—Scripture taken from the *New King James Version.* Copyright © 1979, 1980,
1982 by Thomas Nelson, Inc. Used by permission. All rights reserved.

Library of Congress Cataloging-in-Publication Data
Savelle, Jerry.
Prayer of petition : breaking through the impossible / Jerry Savelle.
p. cm.
ISBN 978-0-8307-5660-5 (hard cover)
1. Prayer—Christianity. I. Title.
BV215.S28 2011
242'.72—dc22
2010041845

Rights for publishing this book outside the U.S.A. or in non-English languages are
administered by Gospel Light Worldwide, an international not-for-profit ministry.
For additional information, please visit www.glww.org, email info@glww.org, or write
to Gospel Light Worldwide, 1957 Eastman Avenue, Ventura, CA 93003, U.S.A.

To order copies of this book and other Regal products in bulk quantities,
please contact us at 1-800-446-7735.

DEDICATION

To my wife, Carolyn, who has stood faithfully
by my side in this ministry and whose prayers have made
me the man that I am today.

To my daughters, Jerri and Terri, who were willing to
give their father to the world in order that I might
fulfill the call of God upon my life.

To my partners, who have believed in me and have helped me go
to the four corners of the earth with the message of faith.

To the Reverend Kenneth Copeland, who first taught
me how to pray the prayer of petition.

And to my Lord and Savior Jesus Christ, who has
entrusted me all these years to take His love to lost
and hurting people all over the world.

CONTENTS

ACKNOWLEDGMENTS

I have always believed that if your vision is truly from God,
then it will be too big for you to fulfill it alone.

I wish to thank all of my staff at Jerry Savelle Ministries
and Heritage of Faith Christian Center, both here in America
and abroad, for their passion, their talents, their giftings and
anointings, and for their deep commitment and dedication
to the call of God upon my life.

You make my job easier, and you bring great joy to my heart.

INTRODUCTION

I've got some exciting things to share with you about prayer. You might be facing an impossible situation today. You might be praying for healing in your body. You might be praying to get out of debt. You might be praying for your wayward teenager. You might even be praying to have a baby. If whatever situation you are praying for looks impossible, I want you to know that God's Word says that "all things are possible." So, my friend, don't ever give up, because prayer changes things.

Many people have never even heard of the Prayer of Petition. Some people may find it too demanding, or a little too specific. Others may find it doesn't fit the small religious box in which they put the topic of prayer. I don't pray because it makes me feel spiritual or so I can be holier-than-thou or because it makes me look or feel good. I pray to get results. Friend, I believe in the power of prayer, and I also believe that the Bible teaches us scriptural principles that we can apply to get results in our prayers sooner than we think.

In Ephesians 6:18, the apostle Paul told us to pray always. I want to encourage you today, and as you continue to read this book, to learn how to apply the Prayer of Petition to your situation, to never give up in prayer. Your attitude should be to pray always.

No matter what the situation is,

no matter how impossible it looks,

no matter how many other people before you have failed,

no matter what the natural circumstances look like,

no matter if it didn't work before,

keep on praying!

I learned about the power of prayer and, specifically, the Prayer of Petition early on in my ministry. I started out in 1969, and kept notebooks of the revelations God showed me regarding prayer. Recently, I was looking at the first notebook I kept from 1969 to 1972. I was a young believer then. I had just given my heart to the Lord on February 11, 1969, and I already had a lot of impossible-looking situations in my life.

I went into the ministry after having shut my automotive business down, but I still had a lot of debt from my company. In the natural, there was no way I could pay back everything I owed. It was too much money. I didn't know what I was going to do. I was bound by my lack of finances, and I felt hopeless. I couldn't fully focus on my new ministry with the looming bills that were piling up on my desk and the many phone calls I was getting from bill collectors who called me at all hours of the day.

If there was anything I needed to learn right then it was how to pray. At the time, I didn't know much about prayer. I certainly didn't know the things that I'm going to share with you in this book. But I was desperate. I needed a miracle. I needed help.

I didn't know where else to turn, so I turned to the best resource—the Bible—and I began to study what it says about prayer. I didn't learn about this topic on my own. I also had the help of godly men like Kenneth Copeland, Kenneth Hagin, Oral Roberts, and T. L. Osborne. I got my hands on everything they had to say about prayer. I was determined to learn how to pray.

The first thing I noticed was that it wasn't important how I sounded when I prayed. I don't know about you, but I don't speak Elizabethan English. There are many religious-minded people today who think you have to pray using "thees" and "thous." I wanted to pray not to sound good to God, but to get results. In my study of God's Word, I quickly learned that I could talk to Him just like I could talk to anyone else. I'm a country boy from Louisiana, and you know what I found out? God knows how to talk country. That's right! He can speak Louisianan! I want to encourage you to approach God in your prayer as yourself. Don't act like anyone other than who He created you to be.

As I devoted my time to learning about the best way to pray, I found out the quickest way to get results from an impossible situation was through the Prayer of Petition. This is nothing more than a formal request that you create and write down based on facts found in God's Word about His will. It's a prayer that you present before God that you took the time to carefully and diligently prepare. It's a prayer that you offer in confidence and in thanksgiving. It's a prayer that brings about powerful results.

When I crafted my Prayer of Petition because of my dire financial straits, God came through for me. It worked! The prayer I formed based on His Word came to pass and I got delivered from my circumstances. The same thing can happen for you!

Now, this is important: Somewhere along the line, I stopped praying this way. I quit preparing my Prayer of Petition the way God had taught me to. Maybe I got too busy. Maybe I was in too big of a hurry. Who knows exactly why? The bottom line was, I was no longer getting the kind of results I used to get when I carefully and studiously constructed a Prayer of Petition.

A year or two before I started writing this book, my wife, Carolyn, told me the Lord had been speaking to her. He said that we needed to go back and start praying like we used to. So one day we both began to do just that. It's amazing what happens when you get back to the basics and revisit an act that once worked. You know what you'll find? It still works! So many of us forget this basic principle. Sometimes when we try something again that was once successful, we think we've stumbled upon something new.

"Look at this," we marvel in amazement. "I did this new thing, new move, or new procedure and look at all the great things it did for me." God knows it's nothing new. He tells us, *Child, you found that truth a long time ago. You just let go of it.* I don't want any of you to forget the truth of the Prayer of Petition. You can never quit praying like this. Stick with it. It works!

I'm excited that you have decided to join me on this journey toward experiencing greater miracles in your life than you have ever experienced before. It's time to get your prayers answered. No matter how bad your situation looks, no matter how impossible, no matter how bleak, no matter how depressing, know that all things are possible. God can perform the miraculous and turn your circumstances around.

If you are struggling financially because of the economy . . .

If you don't have enough money to pay your bills . . .

If you are having a tough time in your marriage and it seems you are heading for divorce . . .

If you are in need of healing . . .

If you have kids who are doing things they shouldn't be doing . . .

Be encouraged! There is hope. It's time you learned how to pray the Prayer of Petition and watch God divinely operate in your impossible-looking situation and bring about His best for your life.

CHAPTER 1

GOD IS YOUR SOURCE

The kind of prayer that the apostle Paul instructed us about and that is the topic of this book is not religious praying. This is not a pious or do-gooder exercise or a formality. Now don't get me wrong, it's definitely a good thing to have a regularly scheduled time of prayer. It's especially great to start your day off early and spend time in prayer before you do anything else.

But you've got to be careful that you don't just spend time in prayer early in the morning only because you feel obligated or just because it's the religious thing to do. This is how Satan can get us into bondage. Prayer can become meaningless and have no power if we do it just to do it.

We must want to learn how to pray, because God has called us to pray. Jesus said, "My house shall be called a house of prayer" (Matt. 21:13, *NKJV*). If there's one thing the Church has got to be known for, it's prayer. And if the Church is known for prayer, it should also be known for its results. It's one thing to just pray all the time, but it's another thing when we start seeing results from our prayers.

Before we pray, we should understand a few things first. We must believe that prayer gives us the ability to do something about whatever we're going through. We must believe that we have the authority to pray. We must believe that prayer can change things and that we can't change any of these things in our own strength. Remember, Paul tells us to "be strong in the Lord, and in the power of His might" (Eph. 6:10, *NKJV*). We don't have any strength or might outside of God. We can't depend on ourselves or on the eloquent words we use in our prayer or on how smart we are. We have to depend on God showing up and working through us to make change happen.

Before we even begin to prepare the Prayer of Petition and unleash the power of God in our lives, we have to remember who our Source is. This principle truth is the foundation for the Prayer of Petition. If you don't understand that God is behind it all, you are not going to be successful in your prayer life.

The first verse of the Bible reveals to us that God is the Source: "In the beginning God . . ." (Gen. 1:1, *NKJV*). He is the origin. He is the reservoir. He is the fountain from which it all flows. The reason we petition God is because He is the Source of our needs being met. When there is nothing that others can do to help, God is our Source. When we are stuck in a seemingly impossible situation, God is our Source. When we've run out of hope on our own, God is our Source.

I love what it says in Psalm 62:5: "My soul, wait thou only upon God: for my expectation is from Him." *THE MESSAGE* puts it this way: "God, the one and only—I'll wait as long as he says. Everything I hope for comes from him, so why not?" Isn't that awesome? Everything you hope for comes from God. *Everything!*

When Carolyn and I started out in ministry 40-plus years ago, we had to learn how to rely on God for everything. I can look back over that long period of time and say with deep conviction that everything we have today—from the house we live in, to the clothes we wear, to the cars we drive—has a testimony behind it. When we shut down my business before I committed myself to serving God full-time, we didn't have a dime to our name. I couldn't depend on my business for a paycheck because I had closed the shop shortly after I invited Jesus into my heart.

I didn't have anyone I could look to for help as far as finances were concerned. Sure, I could have gone to my mom and dad or to

Carolyn's parents and asked to borrow money, but I wanted to prove that God was our Source. The Bible told me that "my God shall supply all [my] needs according to His riches in glory by Christ Jesus" (Phil. 4:19, *NKJV*). If God's Word was true, then He would provide us with whatever we needed. I like what Kenneth Hagin used to say: "Let's just act like the Bible's so."

So Carolyn and I went on a journey of discovery. We were on a mission. We were learning to live by faith. We were learning to trust God. I want to tell you that I have over 40 years of proof that God has never let us down. He has never disappointed us one time. God has answered all our prayers because we learned to pray them according to His will. He has been our Source all these years. Not only has He met our needs, but He has blessed us and enabled us to be in a position to help meet the needs of other people until they, too, can discover God as their Source.

Don't Depend on Others

Maybe you have relied on people or other things in the past to be your source. Maybe you think, *Well, I can always go to Uncle John to help me.* What if Uncle John gets laid off? *Well, I can always ask my boss for help.* What if your boss has problems of his or her own? *Well, I've got a stable job that will give me security for the next 30 years.* What if you lose your stable job?

I don't know about you, but I would much rather depend on God as my Source than people or things, because the true Source never runs dry. I can't tell you the number of people in the last 40-plus years who have promised to do something for me or my ministry but they never came through. I'm sure they meant well, but it just never happened.

I've also had people come up to me and indirectly try to discourage me in my faith by saying, "Well, you never know what God is going to do." Actually, I do know what God is going to do. He's going to come through for me. He is faithful. I know God; it's people I can't figure out! That's the reason I don't make others my source. If someone comes up to me and tells me, "I'm going to give you $100,000 to go toward your ministry and that new building you want to build," I do not go out and order material based on what he says.

Can God use other people to fulfill your need? Of course! But I want to make clear that if other people don't obey what God is telling them to do, God is not limited by their disobedience. It doesn't mean your need won't get met.

I read a newspaper article one time about a little town that had been around for more than 100 years. Now when you think of something that's been around for more than a century, you probably think it'll be around forever. Not so. This particular town shut down. It had no reserves left. The community does not exist anymore. The treasurer of the town stole what little it had left and took off. Businesses closed and members of the community moved away. There is no town there anymore.

My point is, don't depend on what man says about being around for a long time. The psalmist wrote, "God is our refuge and strength, a very present help in trouble. Therefore we will not fear, even though the earth be removed, and though the mountains be carried into the midst of the sea; though its waters roar and be troubled, though the mountains shake with its swelling" (Ps. 46:1-3, *NKJV*). In other words, you shouldn't care if the earth is moved or if the mountains fall into the sea. Why? Because you are linked to the Source—who is an ever-present refuge in times of trouble.

It doesn't matter what man says. It doesn't matter what CNN says. It doesn't matter what the *Wall Street Journal* or any other newspaper says. It doesn't matter what your neighbors say. It doesn't matter what the economy looks like. It doesn't matter what your job forecast looks like. It doesn't matter what the health report looks like. God is your Source; and if you are linked up with Him, then you have every right to be confident that He will come through for you.

Don't Depend on Yourself

When you find yourself in a situation where you are pressed beyond measure and you don't know where to turn, don't trust in yourself. In the natural, you are limited to what you can think up as a solution. Most of the time, what you think up won't work anyway.

This is what Paul was talking about when he said, "For we would not, brethren, have you ignorant of our trouble which came to us in Asia, that we were pressed out of measure, above strength, insomuch that we despaired even of life: But we had the sentence of death in ourselves, that we should not trust in ourselves, but in God which raiseth the dead: Who delivered us from so great a death, and doth deliver: in whom we trust that he will yet deliver us" (2 Cor. 1:8-10).

Paul learned a valuable lesson in his situation. He was under so much pressure and thought he was going to lose his life, but he made the decision not to look to himself. He made the decision to trust God, his Source.

Sometimes you may feel like you have been waiting on God for too long and you need to get involved in your situation and find your own way out. Don't do it. Don't feel like you need to help God. Don't start leaning on the arm of the flesh. God doesn't need our solutions or our help. He needs our faith and obedience. Many years ago, Ford Motor Company used to have the slogan, "Ford has a better idea." Sometimes we think we're Ford. God tells us to trust Him as our Source, but we tell Him we have a better idea. We have to stop trusting ourselves and start trusting the Source.

I remember when Carolyn and I were first learning this truth. Shortly after we were married in 1966, I had joined the National Guard because a friend of mine said I could earn some extra money. I had been in for a short period of time when I was told that our unit might have to go to Vietnam. I shipped off to Fort Dix, New Jersey, for basic training and then for AIT (Advanced Individual Training). When I left, Carolyn was expecting our first child. In fact she was due to deliver just a few days later.

There I was, training, with a wife back home and a daughter who was actually born while I was in boot camp; as a matter of fact, my little girl was three and a half months old before I ever saw her. Carolyn was at home praying that I wouldn't have to go to Vietnam. I'll be honest. I didn't want to go either. It's not that I didn't want to serve my country; I just didn't want to leave my family.

I'll never forget sitting in the barracks with my unit on November 17, 1968, the day I was told that I was supposed to ship out. We were waiting with our duffel bags packed, anxious and nervous. We sat there all day and all night and no one ever came for us. Finally, we went to sleep.

The next morning we found out that the governor of Louisiana was sending our unit back home to train with the state police for riot control (this was all happening during the civil rights movement). I watched buddies that I trained with ship out to 'Nam while my unit went back to Shreveport and started training with the state police. Carolyn and I were so happy that God heard our prayers and kept me stateside. I could still go back to work and attend classes at college in the evenings; I just had to be available to the National Guard whenever they needed me. I knew at any moment they could call me up and tell me I needed to be in Lake Charles, Baton Rouge, New Orleans or some other city. I wouldn't be able to tell them no. I would have to go.

In the summer right after I shut my business down and was preparing for ministry, I got a phone call from the National Guard. It was one of the worst times in my life. I was told to report to Fort Humbug, and that was it. I didn't know how long I would be gone. I didn't have a dime to my name at the time, and I had bills, both business and personal, and a mortgage to pay. I also had a wife and now two babies to feed.

I remember the day I had to leave. I put on my fatigues, grabbed my duffel bag, and walked into the living room. I saw Carolyn sitting on the couch holding my two little girls. She had the saddest look on her face. When I saw her, my heart broke. I walked out of the living room and into the bedroom, took my fatigues off and threw the duffel bag in the corner. The Lord spoke to me, "What are you doing?"

"I can't go," I told Him. "Did you see how my wife looked at me? I can't leave her like that. I can't leave my two babies like that."

He was firm. "You took an oath and committed to the National Guard, Jerry. They said they needed you, and you have to go. Now put your clothes back on, pack your duffel bag and get down to Fort Humbug. I will take care of your family." God then brought to my mind a passage of Scripture I had read just a few days before.

Therefore I say unto you, Take no thought for your life, what ye shall eat, or what ye shall drink; nor yet for your body, what ye shall put on. Is not the life more than meat, and the body than raiment?

Behold the fowls of the air: for they sow not, neither do they reap, nor gather into barns; yet your heavenly Father feedeth them. Are ye not much better than they? Which of you by taking thought can add one cubit unto his stature? And why take ye thought for raiment? Consider the lilies of the field, how they grow; they toil not, neither do they spin: And yet I say unto you, that even Solomon in all his glory was not arrayed like one of these.

Wherefore, if God so clothe the grass of the field, which to day is, and to morrow is cast into the oven, shall he not much more clothe you, O ye of little faith? Therefore take no thought, saying, What shall we eat? or, What shall we drink? or, Wherewithal shall we be clothed? (For after all these things do the Gentiles seek:) for your heavenly Father knoweth that ye have need of all these things.

But seek ye first the kingdom of God, and his righteousness; and all these things shall be added unto you. Take therefore no thought for the morrow: for the morrow shall take thought for the things of itself. Sufficient unto the day is the evil thereof (Matt. 6:25-34).

In other words, He was telling me that God is my Source. The Lord spoke to me again, "Stand in front of your family and start acting like I'm your Source. You tell your wife that I am your Source and she will receive what you're saying." I was quick to obey.

I dressed again, threw my duffel bag over my shoulder and walked back into the living room. "Carolyn," I told her, "I don't have a clue how God is going to take care of you and the girls. I don't know how long I'm going to be gone. I don't have any money. All I know is that God told me not to worry, and that He is our Source and He's going to take care of you somehow."

She looked at me and smiled. "Jerry, I know that. And I also know you have to go, so you don't worry about us. I know God will take care of us. I don't know how He's going to do it either, but I do know you have to go, and there's no two ways about it. Go fulfill your duty and don't you have a second thought about us, because God is going to take care of us. He is our Source." I kissed her, grabbed my duffel bag and started walking to the back door. Before I could reach the knob, I heard a knock.

I opened the door and a man was standing there. He said, "Jerry, where are you going?"

"To Fort Humbug," I replied. "And after that I haven't got a clue."

"Well, how long are you going to be gone?"

I shrugged my shoulders. "I have no idea."

The man looked straight into my eyes and said, "Well, I'm glad I got here before you left. God told me to bring you some money this morning, and it was only just now that I have been able to get over here." He put some cash in my hand and said, "So please take this."

I was stunned. He walked to his truck and drove off so fast I barely had time to thank him.

I took the money to Carolyn and told her, "See, God is our Source." My beautiful wife took my hand and said, "I told you, Jerry, God is our Source."

That incident, at the beginning of our walk of faith, proved to us that God was our Source and that we only had to look to Him. How He went about meeting our need was not our problem to figure out. It was His business. Our only business was to believe that He could and that He would provide for us.

Depend on the Source

Ephesians 3:20 tells us that God "is able to do exceedingly abundantly above all that we ask or think, according to the power that works in us" (*NKJV*). This verse tells me that no matter how big our need is, our Source is bigger than that. I love how this text reads in the *Amplified Bible*: "Now to Him Who, by (in consequence of) the [action of His] power that is at work within us, is able to [carry out His purpose and] do superabundantly, far over and above all that we [dare] ask or think [infinitely beyond our highest prayers, desires, thoughts, hopes, or dreams]."

I want you to know that the Source is bigger than your dreams, your hopes, your thoughts, your needs. As a child of God, you are not limited to what is going on in the natural world. You have a Source who is linked together with you. He is capable of putting you in position where you don't need help from others or from yourself. God will be all that you need.

I like what Deuteronomy 33:27 says: "The eternal God, he is thy refuge, and underneath are the everlasting arms." "Eternal" means forever. What is that verse assuring us of? That we can always depend on God no matter what's going on around us because the Source is eternal. The apostle Paul picked up on this verse when he wrote, "Now unto the King eternal, immortal, invisible, the only wise God, be honour and glory for ever and ever. Amen" (1 Tim. 1:17).

Paul reiterated the truth that God will always be there no matter what we go through. No matter what our nation may go through. No matter what's happening around us. We can have confidence knowing that the Source from whom all blessings flow will be there for us.

I'm telling you, there's never been a time when it has been more important that you learn to look to God as your Source than right now. Some of the greatest financial institutions in our nation are crumbling. Even our government is showing signs of instability. You can't depend on banks, the state or anyone else for that matter. You have to learn how to depend on God.

Build Your Faith

I want to encourage you and give you an exercise that you can use to remember who your Source is. This is especially important as you journey through the Prayer of Petition and start believing God for your way out of impossible situations.

Second Corinthians 1:3 tells us, "Blessed be God, even the Father of our Lord Jesus Christ, the Father of mercies, and the God of all comfort." The *Amplified Bible* says, "Blessed be the God and Father of our Lord Jesus Christ, the Father of sympathy (pity and mercy) and the God [Who is the Source] of every comfort (consolation and encouragement).” In this particular verse, Paul is referring to the Source of comfort and encouragement. But it also implies that God is the Source of everything that we could possibly ever need.

I read this one time during my study time, when I was out in California preaching in a couple of different churches. I was sitting in my hotel room in Anaheim, and I tell you the Holy Spirit came all over me. I was running around the room, shouting and praising God, when this thought came to me: *For every verse I read for the rest of the day that has the words “God,” “Lord,” “Jesus,” “Him,” “He”—absolutely any reference to my heavenly Father—I’m going to say out loud “my Source” immediately after those words.* I wanted to see what it would do for my faith. Let me give you an idea of some of the things I read.

- “But my God [my Source] shall supply all your need according to his riches in glory by Christ Jesus” (Phil. 4:19).

- “Let us therefore come boldly unto the throne of grace [God, my Source]” (Heb. 4:16).

- “Is anything too hard for the LORD [my Source]?” (Gen. 18:14).

I want to encourage you to take some time and study the Scriptures this way. Read them out loud and insert “my Source” in the verses. Let those words sink deeply into your heart. Let them penetrate your mind. Let them build up your faith that God is your Source of supply.

If you keep doing this, you are going to become so “God is my Source-minded,” you will no longer worry. You will not get depressed. You will not fear. You will start to experience an expectancy rise up on the inside of you. While everyone else is worrying and trying to figure out what they are going to do, you are going to be walking with a dance in your step and a smile on your face.

As you spend the next few days or weeks preparing your Prayer of Petition, never forget who your Source is. This knowledge should make you unshakable from this moment forward. No matter what's going on around you, no matter what's happening in the natural, know that God is your refuge. He is your safe place. He has not forgotten your name. He has not forgotten your address. And He has not forgotten how to do the miraculous in your behalf. He is your Source!

CHAPTER 2

The Prayer of Petition

I am going to make you a promise. The Prayer of Petition will enhance and energize your prayer life. It will change you. It will make things happen. It will bring you to places that you never could have otherwise gone. You know as well as I do that if there is anything the Church needs right now it's an energized prayer life that brings results. The fact is, there are some things that are happening in the spirit world right now that will never manifest in the natural if they are not birthed in prayer. Are you ready for it?

Let's get down to some fundamentals. The Prayer of Petition is a prayer supported by evidence and facts based on the known will of God through His Word. It is based on the apostle Paul's writing in Ephesians:

> Finally, my brethren, be strong in the Lord, and in the power of his might. Put on the whole armour of God, that ye may be able to stand against the wiles of the devil. For we wrestle not against flesh and blood, but against principalities, against powers, against the rulers of the darkness of this world, against spiritual wickedness in high places.
>
> Wherefore take unto you the whole armour of God, that ye may be able to withstand in the evil day, and having done all, to stand. Stand therefore, having your loins girt about with truth, and having on the breastplate of righteousness; and your feet shod with the preparation of the gospel of peace; above all, taking the shield of faith, wherewith ye shall be able to quench all the fiery darts of the wicked.

And take the helmet of salvation, and the sword of the Spirit, which is the word of God: Praying always with all prayer and supplication in the Spirit, and watching thereunto with all perseverance and supplication for all saints (Eph. 6:10-18).

Prayer Weapons

There are three major weapons that you and I have access to when we pray: the name of Jesus, the Word of God, and the Holy Spirit. These weapons are not carnal, but spiritually strong enough to pull down strongholds and change what seems to be impossible into possible. Are you facing an impossible situation today? I want to remind you of the weapons you have in your arsenal to use in your Prayer of Petition.

- *The name of Jesus.* Just think about it. The Bible tells us that the name of Jesus carries power in heaven, in earth and under the earth. It also tells us that every name is subject to the name of Jesus. I don't care what that name is. It may be cancer. It may be financial lack. It may be depression. It may be addiction. If something has a name, then it is subordinate to the name of Jesus.

- *The Word of God.* The Prayer of Petition revolves around praying the Word of God. I will talk about this in greater length in chapter 4, but let me explain a portion of it to you now. When you pray the Word of God, then you're praying in agreement with God's will. Paul ends his spiritual charge in Ephesians 6 by telling us to take the sword of the Spirit, which is "the Word of God praying." That's all one thought. I don't know if you knew this before, but the Word of God can pray. But it needs a vehicle, a voice, someone to speak it out. In other words, God needs us to pray His Word. Not only that, but the best part is that God promised us in Isaiah 55:11 that the Word of God will not return to Him void. That promise guarantees results!

- *The Holy Spirit.* The Spirit of God is like the muscle of God. When you call upon the Holy Spirit, He is the one who causes the Word of God to come to pass and to manifest in your life. He's the One who makes it all happen.

The Prayer of Petition Is Distinct

In verse 18 in the Ephesians text that we are studying, we are told to pray "always with all prayer." The *Amplified Bible* says this a little differently: "Pray at all times (on every occasion, in every season) in the Spirit, with all [manner of] prayer and entreaty." We can gather from this passage that there are different kinds of prayers. I believe that if you don't pray the right kind of prayer in certain situations, you won't get the results you need.

The Prayer of Petition is distinctive from other kinds of prayer. It's used only in specific circumstances and requires specific applications to affect a specific result. It is a prayer that's prayed in faith. It is a prayer that refuses to be moved by what it sees. It is a prayer that will not allow negative circumstances to dictate whether or not you believe that what you prayed will come to pass.

There are three kinds of prayer recorded in the New Testament:

1. The prayer of thanksgiving and praise
2. The prayer of dedication and worship
3. The prayer that changes things, which includes the Prayer of Petition

I don't want you to confuse the three, so I'm going to show you the difference.

It's important to know what to pray in different circumstances. A lot of times people say, "Let's pray." Well, what kind of prayer are we going to pray? It's like saying, "Let's play sports." We have to know what sport we are playing. You can't play football with baseball rules. You can't play basketball with volleyball rules. There are certain rules that go along with each particular sport. It's the same way with prayer.

The prayer of thanksgiving and praise is a prayer where you are offering thanksgiving to God in advance for what you believe He is going to do. You are praising Him in advance for the answer you believe is on its way. I believe the greatest expression of faith is when you can praise God before you ever see anything happen.

The prayer of dedication and worship is a prayer where you are dedicating yourself to God. It involves a different approach from that of the Prayer of Petition. In the prayer of dedication, it is permissible to say to God, "if it be Your will," because you are praying about making a choice to commit to doing whatever you believe God is leading you to do with your life.

Here is an example of a prayer of dedication. When friends of ours felt called by the Lord to move from New York to Texas, they weren't that excited about it. After all, New York was their home and their ministry base. Texas seemed so far away and, well, like a different planet than New York. But the Spirit of God started to deal with them about the move, and they began to pray, "Father, we really don't want to move to Texas. In our hearts, we want to stay in New York. But if it be Your will, we will move."

That's the same kind of prayer of dedication Jesus prayed in the Garden of Gethsemane. "Father, if thou be willing, remove this cup from me: nevertheless not my will, but thine, be done" (Luke 22:42).

Because of their willingness to follow His will, and their humble attitude, God made it clear they were to move to Texas, and God has abundantly blessed their obedience.

The Prayer of Petition, the prayer that changes things, is based on the known will of God or His Word. You don't need to pray, "If it's Your will, God, please heal me," for instance, because the Scriptures already tell us that by His stripes we are healed. So we already know healing is His will.

The Basics

For our study purposes, there are three definitions I want to highlight that characterize the Prayer of Petition. Today's *Merriam-Webster* dictionary defines petition as:

1. An earnest request; entreaty
2. A formal written request
3. Something asked or requested

But Noah Webster, the man who compiled the *First Edition of An American Dictionary of the English Language* (1828), gave this definition:

1. In a general sense, a request, supplication or prayer; but chiefly and appropriately, a solemn or formal supplication; a prayer addressed by a person to the Supreme Being, for something needed or desired . . .

2. A formal request or supplication, verbal or written; particularly a written supplication . . .

3. The paper containing a supplication or solicitation

4. To make a request to; make supplication to a superior for some favor or right

A formal request or supplication. You'll notice in Ephesians 6:18, Paul encourages us to pray with "all prayer and supplication." Those two words are different. They are not one and the same. It's like putting your shoes and socks on; they both have to do with your feet, but they are two totally different objects and have two totally different purposes. I'll cover supplication in the next chapter.

A formal request addressed to a person or group in authority. The person that we're interested in presenting this petition to is the highest authority in the universe, our Father God.

A formal application in writing made to a court or a place of authority requesting judicial action concerning matters therein set forth. I know, I know. That is a lot of legal-sounding jargon. Our ministry attorney, who serves on our board of directors, knows a lot of about legal terms, and he's shared with me that if you'll study the Bible, you'll find a lot of them in there. This has nothing to do with being "legalistic," but being accurate in one's prayer life.

We're going to approach this particular definition just like a lawyer presents his case before a court. You'll learn more about that in chapter 4. There I will show you how you research facts and evidence to build your case—your Prayer of Petition—and present it before the throne of God and ultimately win your case, or get your results. When you prepare your petition with diligence and study, you can have a boldness, confidence and peace that the Judge of all the earth will do what's right.

Are you getting excited yet?

My First Prayer of Petition

Carolyn and I have so many examples of Prayers of Petition that came to pass exactly the way we prayed them. Let me share with you the first one we prayed when I started out in ministry.

You already know how difficult it was for us financially when I first went into full-time ministry. I had no idea how I would get out of the mess I had made. I was pretty discouraged at the time I first started learning about this kind of prayer. I had so much debt that it was impossible to stay ahead in the financial game. I didn't know how I was going to get the money to pay back everything and everyone I owed.

So I went to the Word of God and looked at examples where God met the financial needs of His people. I studied and researched and constructed my prayer. I used Scriptures in my prayer because that is how we pray the will of God, through what He says in His Word.

At the top of the page I wrote "Petition for Debt Owed," and I signed and dated the bottom of the prayer. Here is how it read in my notebook.

Father, I come boldly unto the throne of grace that I may obtain mercy and find grace to help in time of need according to Hebrews 4:16. Jesus said in John 16:23, *"And in that day ye shall ask me nothing, Verily, verily, I say unto you, Whatsoever ye shall ask the Father in my name, he will give it you." Therefore, I come before You with the mighty name of Jesus.*

Your Word states in Philippians 4:19, "My God shall supply all your need according to His riches in glory by Christ Jesus" (NKJV). I have need of [and here is where I inserted the amount of money I needed] *for the purpose of paying off the debts that I owe in my business. I am doing this in order to be in harmony with Your Word, which says in Romans 13:8 that I am to owe no man anything, but to love him. I am asking You in the name of Jesus to supply that need.*

How You do it is not my concern, because right now I cast the care of it all on You, according to 1 Peter 5:7. Father, I know in order to reap a financial harvest I must first sow a seed. I have three dollars. That's all I have to sow in order to put this spiritual law of giving and receiving in operation which is stated in Luke 6:38. You said, "Give, and it shall be given unto you, good measure, pressed down, shaken together . . . shall men give into your bosom." Your Word also states in Mark 11:24, "What things soever ye desire, when ye pray, believe that ye receive them, and ye shall have them."

Therefore, on this day, February the 9th, 1972, at 2:35 pm, I believe my need is met. And I now offer praise and thanksgiving because 1 John 5:14-15 says, "This is the confidence that we have in Him, that if we ask anything according to His will, He hears us" (NKJV). And if I know You hear me, then whatever I ask I know I have the petitions I've desired of You. So therefore, Father, I thank You now even before I can see it. I believe that my need is met. I thank You for it in the name of Jesus.

That was my Prayer of Petition. Fourteen weeks from that date, every debt I had was paid off! I still had needs, but all my old debts were paid in full. How did God do it? Supernaturally. I can't even begin to tell you the miracles that God wrought as a result of my praying this Prayer of Petition.

Don't misunderstand me. I'm not telling you that if you pray this same petition, you'll get the same results, and in 14 weeks your debt will be paid off. I'm just giving you an example of a Prayer of Petition that worked in my case.

Ancient Petitions

Do you know that most of the book of Psalms is made up of the petitions of King David? Notice that someone had to write them down, because they are found in the Bible. Either David wrote them or he had a stenographer who followed him around and transcribed his prayers for him. Either way, his prayers are recorded for a reason. God didn't just make them up. Some historian didn't just make them up.

You need to write them down—this is another important component of the Prayer of Petition that I will explore in chapter 4—so that you can remember them and gain strength from them. For that matter, the Bible is full of written-out prayers. Sometimes we just don't notice them. Let me share with you some that stand out in my mind.

The LORD hear thee in the day of trouble; the name of the God of Jacob defend thee; send thee help from the sanctuary, and strengthen thee out of Zion; remember all thy offerings, and accept thy burnt sacrifice; Selah. Grant thee according to thine own heart, and fulfil all thy counsel. We will rejoice in thy salvation, and in the name of our God we will set up our banners: the LORD fulfil all thy petitions (Ps. 20:1-5).

David is praying this Prayer of Petition, but he is speaking as God. It's as though God is using David's mouth, and through his servant God is saying, "I hear you, David, in the day of your trouble, and I will defend you. I will remember your offerings. I will grant you according to my heart. I, the Lord your God will fulfill all your petitions."

In verse 5, David starts using the pronoun "I." The second half of this Scripture passage is bursting with confidence. When you know something for a fact, you're confident. David has his confidence resting in God. He knows for a fact that God will hear him and save him. He knew that God was his Source.

Now know I that the LORD saveth his anointed; he will hear him from his holy heaven with the saving strength of his right hand. Some trust in chariots, and some in horses: but we will remember the name of the LORD our God. They are brought down and fallen: but we are risen, and stand upright. Save, LORD: let the king hear us when we call (Ps. 20:6-9).

In verses 1-4, David is hearing from God, and step by step he is gaining confidence in God's character and the hope that exists only in Him. This is particularly expressed in verse 4, when David pens that the Lord will fulfill his petitions. In verses 5-9, David is finally sure of his faith and trust in God, and his confidence has come forth full circle. He is practically shouting out, "Yes, it's true. I know God will save me."

I like when David says, "Now I know" (v. 5). That is something we need to say more often, especially after we read 1 John 5:14-15: "And this is the confidence that we have in him, that, if we ask any thing according to his will, he heareth us: And if we know that he hears us, whatsoever we ask, we know that we have the petitions that we desired of him." Wow! I sure hope that encourages you as much as it does me.

Hannah was a woman whose story we find in the Old Testament. She was barren (see 1 Sam. 1:2). She wanted children and couldn't have any, so she petitioned God. "LORD of hosts, if thou wilt indeed look on the affliction of thine handmaid, and remember me, and not forget thine handmaid, but wilt give unto thine handmaid a man child, then I will give him unto the LORD all the days of his life, and there shall no razor come upon his head" (1 Sam. 1:11).

The priest Eli had heard her praying in the temple and approached her. He actually thought she was drunk because her lips were moving but she wasn't saying anything out loud. Hannah, of course, was praying silently. When the priest told her to put away the wine, Hannah cleared the record.

"No, my lord, I am a woman of a sorrowful spirit: I have drunk neither wine nor strong drink, but have poured out my soul before the LORD. Count not thine handmaid for a daughter of Belial: for out of the abundance of my complaint and grief have I spoken hitherto" (1 Sam. 1:15-16). Eli finally understood and told her, "Go in peace: and the God of Israel grant thee thy petition that thou hast asked of him" (1 Sam. 1:17).

I really believe this is the kind of prayer we need to pray to bring about the quickest results in what seems to be totally impossible situations—like Hannah, who desperately wanted to have children but was physically unable to do so. You know what happened to her? God heard her petition and brought about her requested result. "For this child I prayed; and the LORD hath given me my petition which I asked of him" (1 Sam. 1:27).

The apostle Paul wrote down many prayers; sometimes he wrote them himself, and other times one of his fellow students did it for him. "Ye see how large a letter I have written unto you with mine own hand" (Gal. 6:11). He had an enormous need to pray. Paul constantly prayed for the churches he had planted and visited. He was burdened by the care of those people he had led to the Lord, and his epistles speak loudly of the prayers for these people.

Acts 3 tells the wonderful story of how the apostles Peter and John ministered healing to a man who was lame at birth and sat at the Gate called Beautiful. Crowds of people saw what they had done and were amazed. Peter took the opportunity to preach to them and told them the man was healed by the name of Jesus Christ. While these two men were speaking and sharing the gospel, the priests in the temple got wind of what was going on. They were angry and arrested Peter and John that night.

In the morning, the two apostles were taken before the court officials who had to decide what to do with them. On one hand, they knew the healing of the man was true; on the other hand, they were afraid that Peter and John would continue preaching what they thought was propaganda. The court commanded Peter and John never to speak of the name of Jesus anymore and threatened them if they continued to do so. When the members of the council saw their threats were meaningless, they let the two men go.

"And being let go, they [Peter and John] went to their own company, and reported all that the chief priests and elders had said unto them. And when they heard that, they lifted up their voice to God with one accord" (Acts 4:23-24). I want you to know the importance of them lifting up their voice to God with one accord; in the next couple of verses, you can read the Prayer of Petition they prayed together.

The only way that you and I can truly pray in one accord is if somebody creates a prayer and we all pray it together. Evidently, this is not something these folks did on the spur of the moment. They carefully constructed it and searched the Scriptures to find out what God said, and then they took that information and injected it into their petition. This is what a Prayer of Petition is all about—taking the time to prepare a prayer based on the known will of God. Notice what they said:

> Lord, thou art God, which hast made heaven, and earth, and the sea, and all that in them is: Who by the mouth of thy servant David hast said, Why did the heathen rage, and the people imagine vain things? The kings of the earth stood up, and the rulers were gathered together against the Lord, and against his Christ. For of a truth against thy holy child Jesus, whom thou hast anointed, both Herod, and Pontius Pilate, with the Gentiles, and the people of Israel, were gathered together, for to do whatsoever thy hand and thy counsel determined before to be done. And now, Lord,

behold their threatenings: and grant unto thy servants, that with all boldness they may speak thy word, by stretching forth thine hand to heal; and that signs and wonders may be done by the name of thy holy child Jesus (Acts 4:24-30).

Let's dissect this passage of Scripture so you can see exactly what I mean in how they searched the Word of God for their prayer. When they said, "Lord, thou art God, which hast made heaven, and earth, and the sea, and all that in them is" (v. 24), they got that from something Moses wrote. When they prayed, "Who by the mouth of thy servant David" (v. 25), they were picking up something that King David had said. Do you see what they were doing? They were thinking back on the writings of Moses and David to form, not a spontaneous prayer, but a deliberate one—a prayer that is on purpose.

You have to remember that in those days, they didn't have a copy of the *King James Bible* like we have and can turn to today whenever and wherever we want. These people in Acts were actually writing the Bible with their experiences. What they did have were the writings of the old prophets. I know this for a fact because when the people received the Holy Spirit on the Day of Pentecost and some folks were confused as to what was going on (some actually thought the people who were speaking in tongues were drunk!), Peter said, "Ye men of Judaea, and all ye that dwell at Jerusalem, be this known unto you, and hearken to my words: For these are not drunken, as ye suppose, seeing it is but the third hour of the day. But this is that which was spoken by the prophet Joel" (Acts 2:14-16).

How did Peter know what the prophet Joel had said? He had been dead for a long, long time. But someone had written down what Joel had said, and when the Holy Ghost came upon the disciples, they had been in the upper room studying the writings of the ancients. It was the only way Peter could identify what was going on.

Let's continue to explore the Prayer of Petition found in Acts 4. When they said, "Why did the heathen rage" (v. 25), they were referencing what we know as Psalm 2:1, where David wrote, "Why do the heathen rage, and the people imagine a vain thing?" What we read in verses 24-28 is the evidence upon which they based their petition. They returned (spoke back) God's Word to Him in their petition, a prayer based on God's will. Now comes their actual petition: "And now, Lord, behold their threatenings: and grant unto thy servants, that with all boldness they may speak thy word, by stretching forth thine hand to heal; and that signs and wonders may be done by the name of thy holy child Jesus" (Acts 4:29-30).

We know there was a terrific move of God in that place after they prayed (see v. 31). But was their petition granted?

Did God grant them boldness to speak the Word?

Did God use them to heal?

Did God give them the power to perform signs and wonders in His name?

You bet God did! "And by the hands of the apostles were many signs and wonders wrought among the people" (Acts 5:12). See, they expected God to stretch out His hand and heal others through them because they had evidence from His Word and therefore had a right to petition Him for it. They presented their case before God, and God granted them their petitions. You're going to see exactly how you can build your case in preparing your Prayer of Petition in chapter 4; I'm just touching on it a bit here so that you can get an idea of what kind of prayer this is.

The God of the Grants

Looking back at the definitions I gave you earlier, the Prayer of Petition is a formal request or application to God. Have you ever applied for anything? I like to imagine this prayer as me applying to God for a grant. The *Amplified Bible* uses the word "grant" a lot. I like how the *Amplified* translates what Jesus said in the Gospel of John:

> I assure you, most solemnly I tell you, if anyone steadfastly believes in Me, he will himself be able to do the things that I do; and he will do even greater things than these, because I go to the Father. And I will do [I Myself *will grant*] whatever you ask in My Name [as presenting all that I AM], so that the Father may be glorified and extolled in (through) the Son. [Yes] I *will grant* [I Myself will do for you] whatever you shall ask in My Name [as presenting all that I AM] (John 14:12-14, emphasis added).

There are times when I need a grant from the Lord. I need financial assistance from Him, and in my Prayer of Petition, I apply for it based on evidence and facts. I pray the Word of God as I talked about in the beginning of this chapter. I make a formal application to the Judge of all the earth, to the Creator of the universe, to the One who has more than enough.

You know, it's a funny thing. I have never gone to the throne of God making formal application or petition and bumped into you up there. I've never seen you. Matter of fact, I've never seen anyone in there. Why? Because there's no line. There's no waiting room. There's no number you have to hold to secure your position.

There was a time, though, when I thought there was a line and I'd have to wait. I used to imagine at least 4 million people up in God's throne room, all waiting for Him to do something for them. I'd look way up in front of me and see Brother Oral Roberts, Brother Billy Graham and Brother T. L. Osborne, and I'd think, *Boy, God will never get to me. There won't be anything left by the time they get everything they need. By the time I get to the front of the line, I'll probably run into a sign that says "closed."*

I couldn't have been more wrong. I don't believe that nonsense anymore. Hebrews 4:16 tells us that we can approach the throne room boldly. I especially know I can have confidence when I bring before Him my Prayer of Petition. He already knows what I need before I even ask. And why wouldn't He give me what I am asking for? I'm His child. I have right standing with Him. I'm only asking for something that is in His will.

I can promise you this: When you start putting together your Prayer of Petition, you are going to find yourself being divinely directed by the Holy Spirit. He's going to get involved in this. You'll start searching through God's Word, find a Scripture that's relevant to your cause and, all of a sudden, the Spirit will lead you to another one . . . and another one . . . and another one.

He is in this with you. You will start to sense His anointing and have the confirmation that you are on target. And when you start praying this petition, a confidence and a peace will build up on the inside of you. You will be living out God's Word and be the recipient of the "hand" of Providence in your life—in the area of your family, your relationships, your health, your finances and the spiritual condition of those around you.

Earlier, I mentioned something about "supplication." That's just the other component of the Prayer of Petition. In the next chapter, I will show you how they work together.

Sample Prayer of Petition for Healing and Physical Restoration

Throughout this book, I will include some of the actual Prayers of Petition I've prayed over the years, as well as some sample ones for various needs. You can use these samples for yourself or as a model for ones you want to construct yourself. The prayer below concerns healing and physical restoration.

I know that some who are reading this book are struggling with sickness. Some may even have recently received a bad report from the doctor. They might have even been told that it's too late. Nothing can be done about their condition. If this is true for you, then this Prayer of Petition is for you. Believe that God can do the impossible. It is His will for you to be healed (see Jas. 5:15; 1 Pet. 2:24).

Be it known this day, _____, _____ (A.M./P.M.), that I receive the healing of my body. No sickness or disease of any kind has a place in my body, so Father, in the Name of Jesus, I come boldly to the throne of grace, and present Your Word.

According to John 16:23, Jesus said, "I assure you, most solemnly I tell you, that My Father will grant you whatever you ask in My Name" (AMP).

In Isaiah 53:4-5, it is written, "Surely He has borne our griefs (sicknesses, weaknesses, and distresses) and carried our sorrows and pains [of punishment], yet we [ignorantly] considered Him stricken, smitten, and afflicted by God [as if with leprosy]. But He was wounded for our transgressions, He was bruised for our guilt and iniquities; the chastisement [needful to obtain] peace and well-being for us was upon Him, and with the stripes [that wounded] Him we are healed and made whole" (AMP).

I declare, according to Matthew 8:17, "He [Jesus] fulfilled what was spoken by the prophet Isaiah, He Himself took [in order to carry away] our weaknesses and infirmities and bore away our diseases" (AMP).

I am redeemed from the curse of the law, which includes all sicknesses (see Deut. 28:58-61), for it is written that Christ purchased my freedom, redeeming me from the curse of the law by Himself becoming a curse for me, for it is written in the Scriptures, cursed is everyone who is crucified so that by my receiving Christ Jesus, the blessing promised to Abraham might come upon me (see Gal. 3:13-14).

I believe in my heart and declare with my mouth that by His wounds I have been HEALED, as it is written in 1 Peter 2:24!

And I thank You and praise You for healing me of _____ _____, and I thank You for making me WHOLE! (see Luke 17:10-19).

_____   _____

(Signature)   (Date)

CHAPTER 3

Supplication

W hen I talk about the Prayer of Petition, the word "suppli-cation" is inclusive in its meaning based on the passage of Scripture in Ephesians. When Paul told us to pray "always with all prayer and supplication" (Eph. 6:18), he had a distinctive pur-pose in using the word "supplication." He wouldn't have used that word if it were just another synonym for prayer. Let's find out what is so special about supplication.

What "Supplication" Means

When I took the time many years ago to really dig through the con-cept of the Prayer of Petition, I had to do a lot of research, especially as it concerned supplication. I'm one of those people who would rather look up something than assume I already know what it means. In my study, I found three definitions of this word:

Supplication: (1) An urgent petition, (2) to make an earnest request, (3) an entreaty.

I knew what an "urgent petition" was, but I wanted to explore the second definition, in particular the word "earnest," a little fur-ther. This is what I found:

Earnest: (1) Intent and direct in purpose, (2) of a serious or important nature, (3) with serious intent or determination.

This supported the notion that supplication is clear-cut and def-inite. It's never a general prayer like, "Dear Father, please bless such and such and be with them, Lord. Amen." And it's also not something you ramble off the top of your head. Supplication is earnest—direct and to the point. I continued to excavate the meaning of these words and was struck by the definition of entreaty:

Entreaty: to beseech with great intensity.

From studying these definitions, it quickly became obvious that the Prayer of Supplication is of a very serious nature. You're not playing church with this prayer. Its significance and weight run along the same line as a petition. They both require preparatory elements to pray to God, just like an attorney has to dig for facts to present his or her case in court.

I believe that one truth about the power of the Prayer of Petition to effectively bring about immediate results in most situations is that God honors the time you take to assemble it. He is touched by your serious determination, the directness in which you bring Him your petition and the intensity of your supplication. It shows Him that you mean business.

In my personal opinion, the Prayer of Petition and supplication puts you into motion. Think of it this way: How many times have you prayed in your morning devotions or before you went to sleep at night, and your prayers seemed to drone on and on instead of being succinct and purposeful?

One of the reasons I advocate praying the Prayer of Petition is because it keeps you away from that kind of mediocrity. It keeps you from being spiritually lazy. It keeps you from just waiting on the sidelines of life, simply hoping that something will happen. When you are intent and direct in your purpose, you are being moved forward in your faith. You are building your faith. As a result, your spirit becomes refreshed. Energized. Inspired.

Peter's Moment of Earnest Prayer

Let's look at some examples in the Bible of supplication—praying earnestly, with great intensity and in specific terms. In Acts 12, we see the persecution of the Church at the hand of Herod Agrippa I, the ruler of Rome. This leader was a pious observer of Jewish law and a ruthless suppressor of minorities.

When, in his mind, people rebelled or spoke out against either the Roman rules or Jewish practices, he deemed them as heretics and persecuted them. To him, the early Christians who were preaching the gospel (like James, who was earlier killed for his beliefs, and Peter) were threats that needed to be eliminated. One day, Herod had had enough of Peter's evangelizing and he arrested Peter during Passover. Herod left him in a prison cell, guarded by a multitude of Roman soldiers.

Herod had every intention of taking Peter's life, but he wouldn't do it during Passover week. It was against his religious principles, and religious people wouldn't do that. So he left Peter in jail until the holiday festivities were over and he could move forward with the execution with a clear conscience. In this passage of Scripture, the scene is set on the day before Peter is to be killed. Peter remained in a prison cell on what was supposed to be his last night on earth.

> Now about that time Herod the king stretched forth his hands to vex certain of the church. And he killed James the brother of John with the sword. And because he saw it pleased the Jews, he proceeded further to take Peter also.

(Then were the days of unleavened bread.) And when he had apprehended him, he put him in prison, and delivered him to four quaternions of soldiers to keep him; intending after Easter to bring him forth to the people (Acts 12:1-4).

From a human perspective and in the eyes of his followers, the Church had seen and heard from Peter for the last time. His ministry was over. His work was finished. He was going to die. If you looked at this situation in the natural, there was no way anything or anybody could free him. He was stuck in that place with no way out. It was a totally impossible situation.

Excuse the drama for a bit, but this was a really serious situation. A man of God was going to be killed if something didn't happen. There is just no way to sugarcoat the predicament Peter was in.

I'm sure you're like me and there have been several times in your life when you have found yourself in a tough position, stuck between a rock and a hard place and unable to move. Perhaps it wasn't a life-or-death situation, but most of us have been trapped in a no-win situation. We have all been in jams where hope is hard to find, where help just isn't coming, where the word "impossible" is written all over the mess we're in.

Some years ago, I was given an ultimatum about our work in Africa. We have fought so many battles with the devil over our ministry in that part of the world; I'm so glad those days are over. But at the time, we were in a bind, and I felt chained to a brick wall. We were told that if we didn't come up with a large amount of money for a particular project we had started, they were going to shut us down. We had a deadline to come up with the money.

I was frustrated to no end. I just couldn't believe what was happening. We had worked so hard for so many years to build that work. We had spent hundreds of thousands of dollars to help the people there. We had sacrificed blood, sweat and tears for this project. And now it was all going to waste? We were on the verge of getting kicked out?

What was even worse was when we found out that part of the reason we were in such a financial tight spot was that Satan had used people from our own ministry there to steal money from our accounts. We instigated lawsuits and were involved in the court systems to fight these people and get our money back, but it didn't matter. The bottom line was the same. We had to pay those folks money by the deadline or lose everything we had worked so hard for. To me, that was a pretty serious situation—almost as serious as the situation Peter was in. My life wasn't at stake, but the lives of hundreds of people who were involved in the great things we were doing there were.

I knew I had some choices. I could take the easy road, lift my hands in surrender, give up and say, "Well, I did my best." I'll be honest. There were some days during this battle when I wanted to do that. I was reminded of the passage in the Bible where Jesus was giving His disciples some detailed instructions before He sent them out to preach the Word. "And whosoever will not receive you, when ye go out of that city, shake off the very dust from your feet for a testimony against them" (Luke 9:5).

I thought maybe this was one time when I needed to do just that. Maybe I needed to let go of the ministry there. Matter of fact, I even had one leg up and was ready to start shaking my foot, but God wouldn't let me. He told me, "I've called you to pull down that kingdom of corruption, so you stick with it. If you don't stay with this project, it's going to set missions back another hundred years." The Holy Spirit continued to speak to my heart, reminding me of my call and encouraging me to hold on a little longer. He pointed out that every good work gets to a certain point where there is a collision with a spirit of corruption. It makes most people frustrated, tired and ready to throw in the towel. Many even give up and quit the whole thing. "Don't let them run you off," God spoke to my heart. "Fight it."

From that point on, my mind was made up. I knew the choice I was going to make. We were going to stand strong and fight, no matter what obstacle, threat or challenge was thrown at us. My goodness, you can't even begin to imagine the opposition we faced! But instead of discouraging me, the problems now began to fuel my energies and caused me to rise up with a determined spirit. I told God, "I've worked too hard and my partners have invested too much into this project for them to take that away from us. I'm not having it." And I petitioned God.

I called my staff together and sat them down for a meeting. I shared my petition with them after I made the statement that we were not going to run out of Africa. I looked at them and announced, "We are not going to be beat. I'm petitioning God for the money that we need by the deadline, and I'm telling you in faith, it will come to pass." I specifically shared with them this message because I wanted to inspire their faith. I wanted them to see that when you construct a specific and direct petition to God; when you make an earnest request; when you beseech Him with great intensity, He will come through. That is the promise of the Prayer of Petition.

I brought my petition before God 11 days before all the money was due. Around 4:00 P.M. that afternoon, I shared the message with my staff. At 11:00 P.M. that same night, by nothing short of a miracle, I received the money and wired it to Africa! One of our partners had been praying for us and said, "God told me to get this money to you today." He went on to say, "It's for your work in Africa."

This all happened around the time I started praying the Prayer of Petition like I used to do years ago. Seeing God work through that impossible situation in Africa encouraged me and reminded me of the inherent power in that kind of prayer. Why I ever quit praying that way is beyond me. I'll say this much, though: Once you start praying like this and start getting results in a matter of hours or days for problems you've been praying about for weeks, months and even years, you learn very quickly to keep on praying in this manner. One thing's for sure, my mama didn't raise no fool, and I'm sure your mama didn't either. I may have temporarily forgotten the need to pray the Prayer of Petition, but I will never forget that need ever again.

Let me be clear. I believe I would not have gotten that money wired over so quickly had I prayed a general prayer like, "God, help us in Africa." I needed to pray something specific, direct and to the point. I needed some definite facts of what I could expect God to do. That is what petition and supplication are all about.

What Happens When You Pray with Intensity

Let's get back to what was happening with Peter in Acts 12. He was sitting in jail, waiting to be executed. I want you to notice what the church did in Acts 12:5: "Peter therefore was kept in prison: but prayer was made without ceasing of the church unto God for him."

In my study Bible, there is a cross-reference by the word "prayer," which leads me to the definition of "instant and earnest." Sounds a lot like the meaning of supplication that I gave you at the beginning of this chapter, doesn't it? I like to read the verse with the cross-reference: "Peter therefore was kept in prison: but *instant and earnest* prayer was made without ceasing of the church unto God for him."

In our modern-day Bible, the translation of "without ceasing of the church" is not a very good one. The English translators interpreted the original Greek word in this text *ektenes,* which means "uninterrupted prayer." If that were true, it would imply that the people of the local church prayed every second of every minute during that time, and that they prayed nonstop for hours on end. The original meaning of *ektenes,* however, means "intent, without ceasing, fervor." It has nothing to do with time. It has to do with the intensity of the prayer (once again, a substance of supplication).

Imagine five runners in the Olympics who are sprinting with every ounce of strength and fortitude in them to make it to the finish line. They all have one purpose in mind—to get there first. As they're running and exerting all of their energy to reach their goal, you can actually see their muscles popping out and the veins in their face and neck jutting out as they attempt to accomplish this physical feat. What is happening? They are all intensely trying to finish first. The folks in the Church who were praying for Peter were stretched out in the intensity of their prayer.

The apostle Paul had a grip on this kind of intense prayer:

For we know not what we should pray for as we ought: but the Spirit itself maketh intercession for us with groanings which cannot be uttered (Rom. 8:26).

My little children, of whom I travail in birth again until Christ be formed in you (Gal. 4:19).

When Paul wrote these words, the "groaning" and "travail" he referred to relate to the things that cannot be spoken articulately. Sometimes you may have something so heavy on your heart that you want to tell someone, but you just can't get the right words out of your mouth. Your feelings are too intense. Your emotions are too strong. You are overwhelmed in your spirit.

When we pray in this powerful way for certain things that we hold dear to our hearts, we have that same kind of intensity. That's when we need the Holy Spirit to help us. Our need is so intense that He needs to step in and get involved in our prayer.

When you are intensely stretched out in the Prayer of Petition, your whole heart is into it. You are not just repeating a prayer you once heard in Sunday School. You are not just reading out loud something you found in an online devotional. You are not getting out of bed half-awake or going to bed exhausted and mumbling some mumbo-jumbo prayer that you can cross off your to-do list.

Your heart is into your prayer. You are praying intensely for your husband to get saved. You are praying intensely for your daughter to get off drugs. You are praying intensely to find the funds to start the ministry God has laid on your heart. You are praying intensely to build a bigger church. You are praying intensely for your son to be healed of leukemia.

You are praying like the church prayed for Peter. They were stretched out in earnest supplication for God to save Peter's life. They knew if they didn't put their whole heart into this prayer, Peter would be dead in the morning.

I've found that when you truly desire something, it becomes easy to imagine yourself having it. When you pray the Prayer of Petition, you are desperate for whatever it is you are asking for. If you are desperate for healing, you will be desperate to create your Petition. If you are desperate for emotional or physical healing, you will be desperate to create your Petition. If you are desperate for a financial breakthrough, you will be desperate to create your Petition.

When you create your Prayer of Petition, you desire it so intensely that it becomes easy to imagine God coming through, and you will not stop praying and believing it until He does. "Therefore I say unto you, What things soever ye desire, when ye pray, believe that ye receive them, and ye shall have them" (Mark 11:24). Notice that desire comes before possession.

Well, God heard the intense longing and desires of the men and women who were praying for Peter, and He answered their prayers. The impossible became possible. While the Church was praying, Peter was sleeping. He wasn't too concerned about dying in the morning. He was sound asleep, but not for long. God woke him up. An angel appeared in his jail cell and unshackled the chains that bound him. This once-imprisoned disciple of Jesus walked out of jail escorted by an angel of God. Talk about a dramatic intervention by the hand of God! It's awesome!

And, behold, the angel of the Lord came upon him, and a light shined in the prison: and he smote Peter on the side, and raised him up, saying, Arise up quickly. And his chains fell off from his hands. And the angel said unto him, Gird thyself, and bind on thy sandals. And so he did. And he saith unto him, Cast thy garment about thee, and follow me. And he went out, and followed him; and wist not that it was true which was done by the angel; but thought he saw a vision.

When they were past the first and the second ward, they came unto the iron gate that leadeth unto the city; which opened to them of his own accord: and they went out, and passed on through one street; and forthwith the angel departed from him. And when Peter was come to himself, he said, Now I know of a surety, that the LORD hath sent his angel, and hath delivered me out of the hand of Herod, and from all the expectation of the people of the Jews (Acts 12:7-11).

Peter walked down the streets of the city and noticed a light on in the home of the disciple Mark's mother-in-law. He thought there must be a prayer meeting going on in there. And there was . . . for him! He knocked on the door and was greeted by a little woman named Rhoda. When she saw Peter standing there, she got so excited. There, before her very eyes, was their answer to prayer. She was so stunned that she didn't even let Peter in the house. She left him standing out by the front door while she ran back to tell the others. The rest of the group could hardly stand it! They didn't believe her at first, but when they opened the door, they saw it was true. It was Peter!

That's what I like about petition and supplication. It seems to get the quickest results in what seems to be impossible situations. We don't know how the answer will come or how God will produce what we are asking for. The people who prayed for Peter didn't give God detailed instructions on how to set him free. They didn't pray, "Dear God, send an angel to open the prison gate, wake him up, walk him out of the place, and send him over here while we're praying." No. They just prayed for Peter's deliverance based upon what they believed was the will of God.

How would you like for some of your prayers to be answered so quickly that you could hardly believe it was true? How would you like to get your miracle of physical or emotional healing? How would you like to get delivered from your financial burden or addiction? How would you like to receive divine intervention in your job, your family or the calling God has put on your heart? The Prayer of Petition, the specific coupling of prayer and supplication, can help you manifest God's will, based on His Word, and bring forth His hand in your life.

In the next chapter, I'm going to show you how to construct a Prayer of Petition. I've been saying all along that this is a carefully studied, researched and thought-out prayer. There are certain steps you need to take to create this prayer that will change your life.

Are you ready to receive what once looked impossible?

Sample Prayer of Petition for Restoring a Marriage

You might have a pressing need for God to restore your marriage relationship. Perhaps you are on the verge of getting a divorce. Perhaps you have found out about your spouse's infidelity. Perhaps your spouse has already left you and you just don't know what to do.

I want to encourage you that no matter how bad your marriage relationship may seem—how broken, how empty, how betrayed—God can restore your union. If this is your situation today, here is a sample prayer you can use for the restoration of your marriage.

Be it known this day, _____, _____ (A.M./P.M.), I receive the restoration of my marriage and family. Father, in the name of Jesus, I come boldly to the throne of grace, and present Your Word.

According to John 16:23, Jesus said, "I assure you, most solemnly I tell you, that My Father will grant you whatever you ask in My Name" (AMP).

I stand on Jesus' words in Matthew 19:4-6: "Have you never read that He Who made them from the beginning made them male and female, and said, For this reason a man shall leave his father and mother and shall be united firmly (joined inseparably) to his wife, and the two shall become one flesh [see Gen. 1:27; 2:24]. So they are no longer two, but one flesh. What therefore God has joined together, let not man put asunder (separate)" (AMP).

I speak the word of truth and I call those things that be not as though they are (see Rom. 4:17).

I pray and confess that my spouse and I let all bitterness, indignation, wrath, passion, rage, bad temper, resentment, brawling, clamor, contention, slander, abuse, evil speaking or blasphemous language be banished from our lives; also all malice, spite, ill will or baseness of any kind. We choose to become useful and helpful and kind to

*each other, tenderhearted, compassionate, understanding, loving-
hearted, forgiving one another readily and freely as You, Father, in
Christ, have forgiven us (see Eph. 4:31-32).*

*Father, it is written in Romans 5:5 that Your love is shed abroad
in our hearts by the Holy Spirit who has been given to us, and I declare that Your love operates without hindrance in our marriage. We
put on love and enfold ourselves in that bond of perfectness, which
binds everything together completely in ideal harmony (see Col. 3:14).*

*In Jesus' name, I declare that we have come to our senses and es-
caped out of the snare of the devil who has held us captive, and hence-
forth will do Your will, which is that we live and conduct ourselves
and our marriage honorably (see 1 Tim. 2:26).*

When appropriate, add the following prayer of agreement:

*Jesus, You said in Matthew 18:19, "Again I say unto you, that if two
of you shall agree on earth as touching any thing that they shall ask,
it shall be done for them of My Father which is in heaven." Therefore, _____ and I set ourselves in agreement, and we believe we receive now, and we praise You for it.*

_____   _____

(Signature)   (Date)

_____   _____

(Signature)   (Date)

CHAPTER 4

Prepare Before You Present

The Prayer of Petition requires diligent preparation. This kind of prayer is not the typical religious kind of praying. It's about actively seeking to know God's will and gathering the necessary information to construct a prayer that gives you the confidence of getting results.

In chapter 2, I addressed one of the definitions of petition: "a formal request" or "formal application." What do those phrases mean? They indicate that much time has been spent in preparation before ever presenting the petition. It takes time. Some of my petitions have taken weeks to prepare.

Have you ever been inside a lawyer's office? Most of them are packed with books of reference material, case studies and court documents. When we were building our house, I told my wife, "Carolyn, I want shelves everywhere. I want my study to look like a lawyer's study." That's because I've got loads of books I use to research the Scriptures, prepare my sermons and pray. I've got more than 25 different translations of the Bible alone. All these books are especially useful when it's time for me to prepare a Prayer of Petition. They help me to build my case. They help me to align what I am asking for with what the Word of God says.

You have to prepare your Prayer of Petition. You've got to have some facts and evidence before the words ever come out of your mouth. Think about it this way. If you want to petition a television station to discontinue airing some filthy program they're showing at prime time, you have to gather together the particulars of what they are doing, why it's wrong and what you are asking them to do about it. You don't just barge into the office, insist on seeing the television station manager and start rambling on and on about God-knows-what. If that's your plan, you'll be escorted out of the building in no time. You can't do that.

You have to build your case. You first have to investigate and re-search why you believe their television shows are influencing others in a bad way. You have to do your homework and find out how young people are being affected, or how their programs are creating more drug use in the schools, or how they are causing an increase in crime in certain areas. Whatever proof you find must be used in your petition. You need to appeal your cause on the basis of pure evidence, not babbling nonsense.

In the same vein, when you go to God about a situation that seems to be totally impossible, you need some facts. You need to know what He says about it. You need to know what promises the Scriptures teach about it. If I have a legal problem and need to get an attorney, I don't want someone representing me who barely has time to meet with me before court. I don't want some lawyer telling me, "Oh, don't worry, I've done this a dozen times. I don't need to hear the details about your case. I'm just going to show up and do what I've done a million times before." No way! I want someone who knows every little detail about my situation. I want someone who has searched through every legal and other necessary resource in order to provide me with a proper case.

When you create a Prayer of Petition, you are just like that lawyer. You start searching. You go on a fact-finding mission. You pray, "Holy Spirit, lead me through the Word of God and show me what God says about my situation." And as you dig deep into preparing this prayer, you will notice that divine direction begins to come. The Holy Spirit shows up and gets involved in your case.

The first thing you need to know in preparing your Prayer of Petition is that you are asking for something in line with God's will.

Know God's Will

The Prayer of Petition is always based on the known will of God. You never pray the Prayer of Petition not knowing the will of God. This is how our heavenly Father contributes to our prayer life. His Word is His part in your prayer. I want you to notice what the apostle John tells us about this:

> And this is the confidence that we have in him, that, if we ask any thing according to his will, he heareth us: And if we know that he hears us, whatsoever we ask, we know that we have the petitions that we desired of him (1 John 5:14-15).

If there is anything you need when you pray it is confidence. You get that confidence when you ask *according to His will*. And when you pray according to His will, you will receive the petitions you are asking of Him. You can't pray the Prayer of Petition without knowledge of His will.

So the big question is, how do you know the will of God? Well, friend, if you've got a Bible, you've got your answer. I'm not saying that the Word will give you all the specific details of His will, like a blueprint, but it will give you the general context. If you are praying about taking a new job in another state, going to a different church or starting a new business, the Bible is not going to tell you what job to take, what church to attend or whether or not to start your own business.

It will, however, lead you in a particular direction and on the trail of finding the definite will of God. Mark my word, there is always a certain passage of Scripture that will shape you into a spiritual mold where you can hear God's specific direction or instruction.

We can know the will of God. God doesn't want us ignorant. Do you know that there are many instances where Paul wrote some form of "Be not ignorant, my brethren" in his letters to the Church? Do you suppose there were ignorant brethren in his day? Do you suppose they have descendants? We are ignorant when we don't study God's Word. We are ignorant when we don't seek out His will. We are ignorant when we don't ask His Spirit for wisdom and guidance.

Here is the best part. You are not alone in this search. As a believer, you have immediate access to the inspiration behind the Bible—the Holy Spirit. "For what man knoweth the things of a man, save the spirit of man which is in him? Even so the things of God knoweth no man, but the Spirit of God" (1 Cor. 2:11). The one who knows the will of God better than anyone lives inside of you! If you take the time to search the general will of God through meditating on His Word, the Holy Spirit will begin to reveal to you the specifics that apply to you as an individual.

Let's get back to the teachings of John. "And this is the boldness which we have toward him, that, if we ask anything according to his will, he heareth us: and if we know that he heareth us whatsoever we ask, we know that we have the petitions which we have asked of him" (1 John 5:14-15, ASV). Notice that the word "petition" is used in this passage. What is the definition of the word according to *Webster's Dictionary*?

- a formal request or supplication
- a formal request addressed to a person or group in authority
- a formal application in writing requesting judicial action

That is the kind of prayer John is talking about. It's a formal prayer. It's not a rush in and rush out prayer. It takes time, effort and preparation to know God's will. If you are the owner of a business and need a loan that looks impossible to get, chances are you would not just run into a bank and ask for a loan. You would not go in there unprepared, not knowing answers to the questions you will inevitably be asked. Can you imagine sitting in front of a loan officer and responding to his questions like this?

"Mrs. Jones, I see you need a loan. Do you have collateral?"

"Excuse me? Collateral? Hmm, I never thought about that."

"How about credit references? Do you have any?"

"Uh, no. I'm sorry. I didn't bring any with me."

No lender would even think about giving you a loan. The fact is, you have zero chance of getting a loan with that kind of presentation—being unprepared, having zero confidence and being totally unorganized. Now imagine what can happen if you walk into a bank with an appointment, having your financial statements ready, and present official documents with proof of your eligibility for the loan. Chances are you'll get that loan.

The same thing applies to discovering the will of God. And don't tell me, "We're not supposed to know His will." If you don't know what God's will is, then the problem isn't God; it's you. Thou art lazy! His Word is His will. Read it, study it, meditate on it and ask the Holy Spirit to guide you through the process.

If you are desperate enough for the results of your Prayer of Petition, you will take the time to do this. I promise you: If you continue living in God's Word and remain in fellowship with Him, He will begin to give you line upon line of His will, one step at a time.

God's Word Is the Final Authority

Let me explain what I'm talking about when I talk about the known will of God. God's Word has to be the final authority in your life. Knowing what His Word says is how you can gather your facts and construct the Prayer of Petition.

For instance, maybe you have been given a recent medical diagnosis that doesn't look too good. Maybe you need healing in your body. Maybe what you are facing in the natural is incurable. Maybe your doctor has told you there is nothing that can be done to make you better. I want to encourage you. Don't ever give up just because someone else said something is not possible. If you go to the Word of God, you'll find that all things are possible. Let God's Word be the final authority in your life. Not your mother's word, not your husband's word, not your boss's word, not your neighbor's word, not your banker's word. God's Word must be the final authority in your life.

Many years ago, I was preaching in a remote area in Kenya, near the Ugandan border. I heard God tell me in my spirit that my father was having a massive heart attack back home in the United States. Well, there I was out in the bush, in the African wilderness, far from home, and nowhere near an airport. Back in those days, there were only a couple of flights a week out of the country that could get me back to the United States in a reasonable amount of time, with one or two stops. The day God spoke to me about my father was on a Saturday.

As soon as the service was over, I headed to Nairobi and made arrangements to catch a flight with several stops that would eventually get me to the United States. There were no direct flights available. I spent days traveling, but it was the best I could do.

As soon as I arrived at the front door of my house, my wife rushed out to greet me. She was in tears and told me what I had already known: "Jerry, your father had a massive heart attack last Saturday night. He was in Florida visiting his brother." So I kissed her and headed back to the airport to catch a direct flight to Florida.

When I got to the hospital, I spoke with the doctors. They were somber and didn't have good news for me. They said it wasn't likely that he would ever leave the hospital. They expected him to die in the next few days. So I went in to see my father.

He was covered in tubes and surrounded by noisy machines. It broke my heart. He was barely conscious. I knelt beside his bed, grabbed his hand, and said, "Dad, the doctors told me the bad news. They say you'll probably die soon, so the way I figure it, we've only got two options. We can either let what the doctors say be the final authority, or we can go to the Bible and let God's Word be the final authority."

On one hand, what the doctors were saying was true. They weren't lying or dramatizing my dad's condition. I saw the X-rays. I saw the medical reports. My father was dying. But on the other hand, I know that Jesus said God's Word is truth. Truth means "the highest form of reality that exists." I continued to allow the Spirit to rise up in me and speak truth into my dad's life.

"Dad, the doctors say you'll never leave this hospital. But I believe in what God's Word says. It says that we are healed by the stripes of Jesus. It says that we are redeemed from every sickness and disease. God's Word tells us to lay hands on the sick and they will recover. Now, I'm basing this prayer on His Word, because I am confident in what it says. So what I want to know, Dad, is if you will agree with me. Will you let the doctor have the final word, or will you let God?"

My dad looked at me with tears in his eyes and said, "Son, let's make God's Word final authority." We prayed, and I want you to know that it wasn't long after we prayed that I was able to take my father home to Fort Worth, Texas.

It's vitally important that we allow this principle to sink in—God's Word is the final authority. We need to know this when we start praying a prayer that will start changing seemingly impossible things. My dad lived another 15 years.

Praying the Word of God

I've already mentioned that the Word of God can pray. This is what the apostle Paul was saying when he wrote, "And take the helmet of salvation, and the sword of the Spirit, which is the word of God: Praying always with all prayer and supplication in the Spirit, and watching thereunto with all perseverance and supplication for all saints" (Eph. 6:17-18). The only thing the Word of God needs in order to pray is a voice. And guess what? We are that voice. I am that voice. You are that voice.

If we didn't have the Word of God, we would have no foundation for faith because faith comes by hearing the Word of

God (see Rom. 10:17). If we didn't have the Word of God, then we would not know what God's will is about anything. Therefore, we would not be able to exercise any faith whatsoever in His doing something for us, because we would have no idea what He said He would and wouldn't do.

This is why the Bible is so important and why God has gone through great lengths to give us access to His inspired Word. Men and women have given their lives so that we could have a Bible in our hands. This precious book has stood the test of time. Time after time, Satan has led revolts against it, and every one of his schemes has failed and will continue to fail in the future.

I'm so grateful to have a copy of God's Word so that I can know what His will is. So that I can believe what He said is mine. So that I can remind Him of what He has said. This is what we do when we pray His Word. We ought to get in the habit of praying this way. This is how we can build a solid foundation for faith.

Don't pray religious things that you've heard someone else pray at one time. There are so many Christians out there who do that. They've heard people praying a certain way and so they mimic those prayers. They don't know why they pray that way; they just do. I think that's the reason "if it be Thy will" got into most people's prayers. Someone heard their grandmother, some preacher or a religious leader say that phrase, and it sounded so spiritual and humble. Guess what? It's not. We don't need to pray "if it be Thy will" when we know what the Word of God reveals about what His will is for us:

- God's will is that we be healed. "But He was wounded for our transgressions, He was bruised for our iniquities; the chastisement for our peace was upon Him, and by His stripes we are healed" (Isa. 53:5, *NKJV*).

- God's will is that we have our needs met. "And my God shall supply all your need according to His riches in glory by Christ Jesus" (Phil. 4:19, *NKJV*).

- God's will is our protection. "For he will command his angels concerning you to guard you in all your ways" (Ps. 91:11, *NIV*).

- God's will is that we have a stable mind free from fear. "For God has not given us a spirit of fear, but of power and of love and of a sound mind" (2 Tim. 1:7, *NKJV*).

One of the first times I ever preached was in Oklahoma City. A man that I met in my hometown of Shreveport was now a pastor and he had asked me to come speak to his youth group. I was excited to do it because I had been studying about prayer and soul winning, so those were the things I preached.

In the evening services, I taught those young adults how to share Jesus with others. Afterwards, I took them out to the streets where we shared the gospel and brought in new converts to the church. In the morning sessions, I taught them about prayer. It was interesting, because at this stage in my ministry, most people didn't want me preaching to the adults; they wanted my message focused on the young people. So wherever I preached, including this church in Oklahoma City, it was almost as if the adults didn't know I was even there.

But something amazing started happening. The youth were on fire. They were excited. Their prayers were being answered. They were talking about it. They were sharing their faith. They were winning people to the Lord. These young people had such phenomenal results from their prayers that the word started spreading around the church. My pastor friend approached me and said, "I don't know what you did or said to our young people, but you sure got them turned on. What are you doing?"

I said, "I'm teaching them soul winning and prayer."

"Well, whatever you're doing here, it's working. And I like it! Listen, our deacon board is having a prayer meeting tomorrow morning; why don't you come and sit in?"

"Thank you, I will," I told him. "It would be an honor."

So I went to the prayer meeting. It began with the head deacon standing up and asking for prayer requests. Immediately, almost every hand went up. I remember one man said, "Brother Joe, a member of the church who has been here for many years is dying of cancer. We don't know why God put that cancer on him. We just don't understand the ways of God. His ways are past finding out." Three or four "amens" rang out in the pews. The man continued, "We just want to remember this brother in our prayers this morning. If it be the will of God to heal him . . ."

Oh boy, I thought, *they already said God put the cancer on him. Now they are saying "if it be the will of God to heal him . . ."*

Another guy stood up and said, "You know the brother that came into the church a few weeks ago, the one who got saved and had a glorious conversion experience at the altar? Well, he didn't have a job when he came in, so we prayed for him and, praise God, the next day he got a job. I just found out he lost that job. We need to remember him again. We don't know why God took that job from him. The

Lord giveth and the Lord taketh away. Blessed be the name of the Lord." More amens.

I'm telling you, after those two prayer requests, I could hardly stand it. I thought to myself, *The young people here would never pray like that.* But I couldn't say anything. I was a guest, after all. The madness went on. One after another, the members of the deacon board stood up and started talking and praying with that kind of religious formality—"if it be Thy will." I couldn't believe it! You know the feeling you get when you're standing somewhere minding your own business and someone starts cussing and using four-letter words with the word "God" in them? It ties a knot in your spirit, and all you can think is, *Get me out of here and fast!* Well, that's exactly how I felt.

The Holy Spirit started working in me. He wanted me to do something I just didn't think I could do. I tried to reason with Him. "If I do what You are asking me to do," I said under my breath, "they are going to ask me to leave. They'll run me out of here! I can't do it. I don't have the authority to do it!"

God refused to listen to me. "That's the reason I had the pastor bring you in," He assured me. "Say it." I kid you not. In that same moment, the pastor stood up and said to the church, "Brother Savelle has been teaching the young people on the subject of prayer." Then he turned to me. "Brother, what do you think about our prayer meeting?" I wanted to sink down in my chair, but the Holy Spirit wouldn't let me.

I took a deep breath. "Pastor, please forgive me for being so blunt. But that is the worst kind of praying I've ever heard in my life!" Every eye was on me. I knew I was in deep trouble. The head deacon had fire shooting out of his eyes.

The pastor was quiet for a minute. Finally he said, "Oh, really?" *Lord, help me*, I prayed. "Sir, please forgive me again. But I know the will of God in every one of those prayer requests that you just prayed."

"Oh you do? How do you know?"

I turned my gaze to the big Bible that sat on top of the pulpit and pointed toward it. "See that book you've got there? That is the will of God. If you read it, you would find the will of God in every one of those situations you just prayed about."

That did not sit well with the deacon board. People started hemming and hawing and murmuring and grumbling. Matter of fact, one woman was so mad she ran to the front of the church and demanded the meeting be over. I found out later it was the head deacon's wife. She glared at me and told the pastor to give me 50 bucks and send me home. They did.

Not long after that, Brother Kenneth Copeland asked me to come work for him and move to Fort Worth. I started traveling with him to his meetings and ended up back in Oklahoma City. My job was to introduce Brother Copeland, turn the tape recorder on and help in the prayer lines. As I stood up to begin the service, my eyes fell on the third row. There sat the head deacon and his wife who had thrown me out of their church a few months earlier.

I thought, *Dear God. They've come to disrupt Brother Copeland's meeting, and it's all because of me.* I could hardly keep my attention on what I was supposed to be doing. I was so relieved when the meeting was over. As Brother Copeland and I were getting ready to leave, I felt a hand on my shoulder. It was the deacon.

"Do you remember me?" he asked.

"Yes, sir, I do."

"Then you remember my wife."

I felt so uncomfortable. "Yes, sir, I do." I expected him to yell at me or something, but he didn't. I'll never forget what he said.

"When you attended our prayer meeting a few months ago, you said some strong things. Honestly, you made me so mad. If it had been legal, I would have hurt you. But you know what I did instead? I went home, got my Bible out and started searching the Scriptures to prove you wrong." A smile came on his face. "Thanks, son, for not compromising your message. It changed my prayer life." He then went on to say, "You're right, the will of God is in the Word of God."

Write It Down

Another key to preparing your petition is to write it down. Understand that this is not a mandatory act. You don't *have* to write it down. This is not a religious formality that will make the Prayer of Petition work. Not at all. I'm just saying that in my experience, I've found that writing this prayer out has benefited me in many ways. It has reminded me of God's promise and it has energized my faith when I needed it most. It is a point of focus.

Not only that, but I can tell you that when I've written down my Prayers of Petition, I begin to notice that it's not just Jerry writing something anymore. The Holy Spirit is inspiring my prayer, and what I am writing becomes holy because He has inspired it. When you get inspired this way, you get to the point where you can hardly wait to pray the prayer.

Some of you may be thinking, *I've never heard of writing out your prayers*. Well, have you ever heard of Romans, Galatians, Corinthians, Philippians or Thessalonians? That's right! Every one of those books was birthed in prayer as Paul interceded for the churches in those cities. In these letters he repeatedly told the Church that he does not cease to pray for them (see Col. 1:9). Writing these letters was Paul's way of praying for these people. This is a great example of how we can follow his lead and pray effectively.

Make It Formal

One of the definitions of petition is "a formal application in writing." Carolyn and I have written out almost every Prayer of Petition we have prayed. When we first moved to Fort Worth, we had to furnish our home. We didn't have much money, or furniture, for that matter, but we believed that God would supply our need. I told my wife, "Carolyn, go into town, look in all the stores, and find whatever it is you want to put in this house. Write down everything you want and price it out. When you have spent enough time and you are satisfied in your heart that you have written down everything you want in our house, bring it to me and I will construct a petition with that list."

A few days later, Carolyn brought the list to me with the prices of each piece of furniture, and I spent several weeks constructing the prayer. We typed it up, dated it and signed it. Just like an official court document. We made it a formal process. Then we prayed it together. I'll never forget the phrase I added to the prayer: "Father, You know these prices are subject to change." And at the moment we prayed, we believed that we received. I told Carolyn, "Every time a piece of furniture manifests, just check it off the list." She did. If you saw that paper today, you would see that every item we prayed for has a little check by it. Our Prayer of Petition came to pass.

Again, writing your prayer out is not something you have to do, but think about it. If something will inspire your faith, wouldn't you want to do it? If something will give you an advantage, wouldn't you want to take it? I know I would! Making a formal application makes it a reality in our spirit. We are not crawling into God's throne room begging Him. We are not coming into His presence on our own merit. We are asking Him for something based on the facts that we have found in His holy Word.

There have been times when I took this formal request so seriously that I wouldn't even pray the petition without getting dressed up. In my mind, I was about to approach the highest authority that exists. It helped me keep my faith running at its highest. I honestly didn't feel right about going into His presence in a pair of Levi's and tennis shoes. I don't go to the bank in a pair of Levi's and tennis shoes. I certainly wouldn't go to the White House in a pair of Levi's and tennis shoes. When I have Kingdom business to attend to, I want to be dressed for the occasion. Now, once again, I'm not saying that you have to do this to pray the Prayer of Petition. It's just what I was inspired to do at the moment in order to have the greatest impact on my faith.

You can be casual if you want to. What matters the most is the state of your heart. I've found that making the petition as formally as possible—whether it means dressing up or even typing the prayer out—helps to activate my faith. You can do whatever makes you feel formal. Maybe you want to pray in a particular room or during a particular time of day or in a particular position. Whatever you do, think about the Prayer of Petition in a formal sense, not just a few phrases you mumble off before you fall asleep at night.

My wife and I have several notebooks filled with Prayers of Petition. Sometimes we have even carried them around with us everywhere we went. They gave us a reference on which to empower our faith. Every time the devil whispered, "This is impossible. It's never going to happen," Carolyn and I would dig into our notebooks and read our prayers out loud. We said, "You're wrong, devil. This is possible. It is written . . ." When you have your written prayer as a reference, you can take it with you everywhere you go and remind yourself (and the devil) of what God said is true.

Point of Contact

Another reason I suggest writing the Prayer of Petition is because it is a point of contact to release your faith. Luke tells the story of a sick woman whom Jesus healed. She saw Him in a crowd and believed that if she could only touch His clothes, she would be made whole (see Mark 5:28). That was her point of contact to release her faith. When the centurion asked Jesus to heal his servant, he believed Jesus could do it simply by saying the word (see Matt. 8:8). That was his point of contact.

Having a point of contact in writing your prayer not only releases your faith, but it also helps you to remember it. How many times have you read something and only minutes later forgotten what you just read? It happens to all of us. God knows this, and this is why He asked the Israelites to write the Word and put it where they would remember it. They actually wore headbands and wristbands that contained the written Word. While you don't have to do exactly that, I recommend doing something, whatever it takes, to keep God's Word, your Prayer of Petition, before your mind and in your thinking.

We once had a young man working for us. I got so tickled at him. He wanted a job traveling with me on the ministry team, but at the time we didn't have any openings. The only position we had available was maintenance work. I asked him if he was interested in that role, and he said yes. On his first day on the job, I was sitting in my office and happened to look out the window. I saw a guy who looked like he had just come from outer space holding a rake and a hoe in his hands.

This young man had a huge cassette tape player (this was before the Sony walkman or the iPod—I believe God may have invented the walkman just for him!) taped to a big leather belt wrapped around his waist. He had huge headphones on—the kind you see radio disc jockeys or audio professionals wear. But there was more. He had a coat hanger wrapped around his neck with a bunch of index cards hanging from it. I found out later he was listening to sermons on his tape player, and the note cards had Bible verses written all over them. I was impressed. There he was, working hard on the lawn and reading and listening to the Word. This man did whatever he needed to do to keep himself immersed in God's Word.

Sometimes you need to be a little creative to keep the Prayer of Petition before you. I love the story of some friends of mine. This couple was believing for a new home. They went to a mortgage company that offered an incredible rate, but there were some requirements they had to meet. While they met some of these requirements, the folks at the mortgage company told them they didn't meet all of them. They were disappointed but prayed and believed God's Word that He would give them the desires of their heart. In this case, it was this particular home.

For some time while they prayed, they didn't hear a single thing from the mortgage company. But they weren't discouraged. In fact, they believed God so much that they started packing up their belongings. They prayed; they packed. But they did not hear a peep from the lender. The devil tried to discourage them. Over and over he told them, "You're not going to get this house." They fought the doubt and said, "Shut up, devil. You're a liar. God already said He will give us the desires of our heart."

One day, the woman saw a vision of a loan document that read they would receive this loan at 6.5 percent interest. She was so excited she couldn't wait to share it with her husband. He could hardly believe it. It confirmed that what they were believing for was going to come to pass. He wanted to take this vision a step further, so they were led to write it down and replicate the vision of the approval document.

This wonderful couple got a piece of paper and began to type out a petition. They wrote, "This application for the loan has been approved by the state of Texas for us at 6.5 percent interest, which will go into effect immediately upon the signing of the mortgage contract." Then they got out a red marker and wrote in big letters, "APPROVED."

Days passed, and though they had several calls from the lender, none of it was good news. Their faith was unshakable. They kept on believing and looked at and read their Prayer of Petition whenever they needed to give their faith a little boost. One day they got a call from a woman at the company. She told them that 8 out of 10 people on the board were against them getting a loan. Things weren't looking good.

My friends didn't give up. They were reminded of the verse that said, "And the LORD answered me, and said, Write the vision, and make it plain upon tables, that he may run that readeth it" (Hab. 2:2). They took out another sheet of paper and made a copy of their petition to post on their refrigerator. They believed that God would be faithful. On the last day of the deadline for their loan, they got a phone call from the same woman who earlier had given them a bad report.

She said, "For some reason, I don't know why, the board has decided to approve your loan. They said yes to you only as a test program. You two got lucky." (We all know it wasn't luck.) Two days later, this couple received a letter in the mail that stated the approval was official. Strangely, the letter from the mortgage company had the word "APPROVED" written out exactly in the same slant as they had written it in their petition! God is good!

This story should excite you. It should encourage you. It should make you want to invest the time to prepare your petition and write it down. When you see a visual of what you are believing for, like my friends did, it will help when discouragement tries to set in. Or when others say no . . . or when the devil says no . . . or when your friends say no . . . or when religious people say no.

Your written Prayer of Petition will remind you that God says yes. And for that, He needs to get all the praise.

Sample Prayer of Petition for Freedom from Addiction

So many people today are struggling with some kind of addiction. It comes in many forms, whether it's an eating disorder, alcoholism, addiction to drugs, pornography or excessive spending. When we are dependent on something other than God, we only hurt ourselves and hinder our relationship with God from being blessed to the fullest.

If you are struggling with an addiction of some kind, I want to offer you a sample Prayer of Petition for your situation. Believe that God can provide your needs. Believe that through God—and God alone—you can find a way to overcome your problems. Believe that God can break the chains of whatever it is you are having a hard time letting go of.

> *Be it known this day, _____, _____ (A.M./P.M.), that I receive Your heavenly grant for my freedom and deliverance from _____ addiction. Father, in the name of Jesus, I come boldly to the throne of grace and present Your Word.*
>
> *According to John 16:23, Jesus said, "I assure you, most solemnly I tell you, that My Father will grant you whatever you ask in My Name" (AMP).*
>
> *I stand on Romans 10:9-10,13. I believe in my heart and say with my mouth that Jesus is the Lord of my life. I also declare that as of TODAY I am free and delivered from _____.*
>
> *According to Ephesians 3:16, I am strengthened and reinforced with mighty power in my inner man by the Holy Spirit who lives and dwells in me. I am strong in the Lord, and I am empowered through my union with Him. I draw my strength from You, Lord, that strength which Your boundless might provides (see Eph. 6:10).*
>
> *On the authority of Matthew 18:18-19, I bind Satan and all his principalities, powers and master spirits who rule the darkness, and*

spiritual wickedness in high places, and declare them unable to op-erate in my life and that I am loosed from their assignments, in the name of Jesus. I will not become a slave of anything or brought un-der its power (see 1 Cor. 6:12), and I cast down any and every thought that tries to exalt itself above the Word of God (see 2 Cor. 10:4-5) in my life.

I cover myself today (and every day) with the full armor of God which You have supplied for me . . . the helmet of salvation . . . my loins are girded with truth . . . I have on the breastplate of righteous-ness . . . my feet are shod with the preparation of the gospel of peace . . . I hold the shield of faith . . . and the sword of the Spirit, which is the Word of God. With God's armor on, I am able to stand up against all the strategies and deceits and fiery darts of the devil, in the name of Jesus (see Eph. 6:10-17).

Thank You, Father, that greater is He that is in me than he that is in the world (see 1 John 4:4); and because He lives in me, I am able to withstand temptation. You always make a way of escape (see 1 Cor. 10:13).

Therefore, Father, I fearlessly and confidently and boldly draw near to Your throne of grace, and I may receive Your mercy for any failure and find Your grace to help in good time for every need. Your help always comes just when I need it (see Heb. 4:16).

Father, I thank You that TODAY I am delivered and free of my addiction to _____. In Jesus' mighty name!

_____   _____

(Signature)   (Date)

CHAPTER 5

Thanksgiving

Giving thanks is a vital part of the Prayer of Petition. God favors people who have an attitude of gratitude. You cannot begin and end this prayer without thanking the One who makes it all possible.

Notice what the apostle Paul wrote: "Be careful for nothing; but in every thing by prayer and supplication *with thanksgiving* let your requests be made known unto God" (Phil. 4:6, emphasis added). I like to read Paul's admonishment in the *Amplified Bible*: "Do not fret or have any anxiety about anything, but in every circumstance and in everything, by prayer and petition (definite requests), *with thanksgiving*, continue to make your wants known to God" (emphasis added).

Paul made it clear. Your prayers ought to include thanksgiving. In fact, it's wise to enter into God's presence with thanksgiving and to make it the first thing that you do. When you meet someone for the first time, wouldn't it be rude to blurt out, "Here is a list of all my problems. I'd like to talk to you about my needs," before you introduce yourself, ask them how they are, and talk with them for a bit? Of course it would! Engaging in introductory conversation is a courtesy and a sign of respect.

God wants the same kind of courtesy and respect. When you go into your prayer closet, He appreciates it when you start off your prayers by thanking Him—thanking Him for who He is and for what He has done. This is part of what it means to "enter into his gates with thanksgiving, and into his courts with praise" (Ps. 100:4). Thanksgiving carries a lot of weight.

When God observes an attitude of gratitude in us, it moves Him. Do you remember the story of the 10 lepers that Jesus healed? Let's read this story.

Now it happened as He went to Jerusalem that He passed through the midst of Samaria and Galilee. Then as He entered a certain village, there met Him ten men who were lepers, who stood afar off. And they lifted up their voices and said, "Jesus, Master, have mercy on us!" So when He saw them, He said to them, "Go, show yourselves to the priests." And so it was that as they went, they were cleansed. And one of them, when he saw that he was healed, returned, and with a loud voice glorified God, and fell down on his face at His feet, giving Him thanks. And he was a Samaritan. So Jesus answered and said, "Were there not ten cleansed? But where are the nine? Were there not any found who returned to give glory to God except this foreigner?" And He said to him, "Arise, go your way. Your faith has made you well" (Luke 17:11-19, *NKJV*).

All 10 lepers were immediately cleansed as they walked away. They acted on what Jesus said and they were healed. But only one of them came back to thank Jesus. Nine out of 10 healed lepers went about their business after the encounter with the miraculous. Only one had enough sense in him to show the Healer gratitude. But there is more to the story.

Notice that Jesus told this man—not any of the others—"Thy faith hath made thee whole" (Luke 17:19). In other words, this man—not any of the others—was not only cleansed, but was also made whole. The rest of the lepers might have been cleansed, but this one leper was made whole. There is a big difference. Whole in this man's case meant that he not only was free of the disease of leprosy, but there was no longer any evidence in his body that he even had the illness to begin with.

As far as the other nine men were concerned, because they weren't made whole, you were still able to tell they had the disease. Leprosy decays the flesh, which means that most, if not all of these men, still had signs that they had once had this disease. Even though Jesus healed them of leprosy, they still suffered from the physical effects of the disease, whatever their physical defect happened to be. The thankful leper was the exception. There was no trace of leprosy anywhere in his body—he was made whole!

Think about your own life. What do you suppose you have been missing by not being thankful? Sure, it's wonderful to be cleansed, but don't you want more than that? Don't you want the full effect of wholeness in your life? Don't you want to experience God doing exceedingly, abundantly above all that you could ask or think (see Eph. 3:20)?

Thanksgiving is a crucial part of the recipe of the Prayer of Petition. It is what "seasons" our prayer. I love turkey and dressing. My wife makes it the best. Even though she is an amazing cook and can make anything taste good, I know that if she left out the proper seasoning, her unique blend of herbs and spices in the turkey and dressing, the dish wouldn't taste as good. I would be able to tell that something was missing.

Don't leave out the "seasoning" in your prayers. I can promise you this: The Prayer of Petition works a whole lot better with thanksgiving.

When you pray, start off by thanking God for what He has already done; and then thank Him for what you believe He will do.

When you do this, not only will God take notice, but it will also do something for you. It will energize you. It will enliven you. It will boost your spirit. Being thankful helps to drive out gloom and doom, especially if you have come to God with a heavy heart.

How many people do you know who start their prayer off being really depressed, and by the time they end their prayer, they're still really depressed? I'm sure you know at least a few. Who knows? Maybe you are one of those people! When you begin to pray the Prayer of Petition and supplication with a spirit of discouragement, you'll probably lose your inspiration.

You get tired, frustrated and disappointed. When you add praise to your prayer, however, and you are moved to thank God for His goodness, mercy, love and grace—just a few things you can be grateful for—it works in your behalf to remove depression, oppression, doom or any other bad thing that tries to weigh you down.

Don't Be So Quick to Forget

The children of Israel had a bad habit of coming to God with a spirit of despair. This happened all the time, even though God provided for them time and time again. What was their problem? They were ungrateful. When God delivered them out of Egypt and they went about their journey toward the Promised Land, they constantly murmured and complained about one thing or another.

They were quick to forget about the miracle of God leading them out of the land of slavery. They were quick to forget about the miracle of God parting the Red Sea so they could pass through to freedom. They were quick to forget about the miracle of God supplying them with manna from heaven every day.

Every time they encountered a miracle, they would get so excited and start praising God. But their enthusiasm wouldn't last long. The minute something bad happened, they didn't stop to think of the wonderful things God had done for them the day or two before. Instead, they complained. And cried. And got mad at God. The Israelites repeated this vicious cycle for a long time. It looked something like this.

When God delivered them from the Egyptian army and the Red Sea, they sang and rejoiced. When they got to the other side, they were thirsty. They lost their song and started talking about dying. God caused water to flow out of a rock. Glory be to God! They got their praise back on. Then the Israelites got hungry, and they started complaining and saying it would have been better for them to stay in Egypt as slaves. God caused manna to fall from the sky to feed them and, what do you know, the people reverted back to shouting, singing and praising. But wait. Soon enough, they realized they were bored with eating manna every day. What do you think they did next? That's right. They whined, complained and grumbled about God not even having the decency to change the recipe.

Reading about the Israelites' experience in the wilderness should help us realize the importance of being thankful. When you find yourself in a seemingly impossible situation, you have to remind yourself about all that God has done in the past, about how He has gotten you out of impossible-looking situations before. When you do this, your impossible situation won't look so impossible anymore. If the Israelites had stopped complaining so much, it could possibly have kept them from wandering around the desert for 40 years.

Take the time to thank God in your prayers. Your faith will become stronger. You will have more joy. And you will have created the perfect recipe for an effective petition.

Be Thankful by Remembering Your Covenant

The apostle Paul was a man of prayer. Most of the books he wrote in the New Testament share some wisdom about how we should pray. I want you to notice some of his prayers and how he seasoned them with thanksgiving. This man of God had the good sense to begin most of his letters to the early Church by thanking God. It was a sign of the prominent place gratitude had in his prayer life.

First, I thank my God through Jesus Christ for you all, that your faith is spoken of throughout the whole world (Rom. 1:8).

I thank my God always on your behalf, for the grace of God which is given you by Jesus Christ (1 Cor. 1:4).

I thank my God upon every remembrance of you (Phil. 1:3).

We give thanks to God and the Father of our Lord Jesus Christ, praying always for you (Col. 1:3).

We give thanks to God always for you all, making mention of you in our prayers (1 Thess. 1:2).

I thank my God, making mention of thee always in my prayers (Philem. 1:4).

Get the point? Do you see how often Paul thanked God? Here's the thing: There are many times he made his praise personal and said *"my* God." I believe it's important that you realize the reason Paul frequently gave thanks this way is because he had based his petition on his covenant relationship with God.

When you accept Jesus as your Lord and Savior, the Bible says that an exchange takes place. This exchange is based on a covenant relationship that is established with God when we are born again. "But now He has obtained a more excellent ministry, inasmuch as He is also Mediator of a better covenant, which was established on better promises. For if that first covenant had been faultless, then no place would have been sought for a second" (Heb. 8:6-7, *NKJV*). We have a covenant relationship with God that is founded on better promises than those of the Old Testament (or Old Covenant). This is what gives us the boldness and the right to approach the throne of God with our Prayer of Petition.

Through this covenant, our old life was exchanged for a new life (see Eph. 4:22-24). Jesus took our sins and gave us His righteousness (see 2 Cor. 5:21). Sickness was exchanged for health (see 1 Pet. 2:24). Poverty was exchanged for prosperity (see 2 Cor. 8:9). Spiritual death was exchanged for eternal life (see John 5:24). In this covenant connection we become God's sons and daughters, and everything God has is ours, and everything we have is God's (see John 1:12; 1 Cor. 3:21-23).

The writer of the book of Hebrews made a point to reflect on this tie that binds us to God. "For this is the covenant that I will make with the house of Israel after those days, saith the Lord; I will put my laws into their mind, and write them in their hearts: and I will be to them a God, and they shall be to me a people" (Heb. 8:10).

When Paul wrote "my" God, the sentiment behind those words was a reflection of intimacy—a close relationship between him and God. It also denoted a confidence, a blessed assurance that whatever he petitioned "his" God for would come to pass because God was "his" God, and they were on intimate terms.

Another example of this covenant element of petition is how Jesus taught us to pray. What else do you think He meant when He advocated that we start our prayers by saying, "Our Father"? He was illustrating how important it is to remember our covenant relationship with almighty God.

I want to show you some examples of prayers and supplications with thanksgiving that speak of covenant. Read the inspiring words of the psalmist: "I will love thee, O Lord, my strength. The Lord is my rock, and my fortress, and my deliverer; my God, my strength, in whom I will trust; my buckler, and the horn of my salvation, and my high tower" (Ps. 18:1-2).

Wow! The writer, King David, began his prayer by communicating the basis of his covenant relationship with God. He was confessing that God is everything that he needs Him to be. There is no way that after repeating those powerful statements, the writer thought for one second that his prayer didn't reach God's throne. Before he even presented his request before God, he articulated who God is. Now that's some powerful stuff!

Earlier in the Old Testament, we have a record of God doing something similar with Abraham. There were many instances where

God told this patriarch who He was. He declared to Abraham that He was Almighty God, El Shaddai, All Superior, All Sufficient—the One who is capable of being anything he needed Him to be.

Maybe you need some encouragement today. Maybe you need God to become more real to you today. I want you to know that, even as you read this book, I believe He is telling you that He is everything you need Him to be. He is your Father. He is your physician. He is your lawyer. He is your provider. He is your counselor. I hope you are encouraged and that your spirit is recharged by these truths. And I certainly hope this gives you more than one reason to thank Him every day of your life.

Let's go back to Psalm 18. In this passage of Scripture, King David acknowledges who God is by writing down that God is his rock, his fortress, his deliverer, his strength, his shield, his stronghold. Notice how faith-filled these statements are.

There was no room for doubt, questions or fear. And when you bring your petitions before the Lord, I want to challenge you to come before His throne room with this same confidence and attitude of praise. Challenge yourself to exercise your faith by reminding yourself that God is your everything. Thank Him for the very fact that He *is*. I can guarantee that when you start building yourself up in this way, you will develop an attitude of gratitude that will deepen your faith and enhance your prayer life.

Let's see what else David had to say: "I will call upon the LORD, who is worthy to be praised: so shall I be saved from mine enemies" (Ps. 18:3). I love how David prayed in this passage. He spoke covenant language in every word he wrote. What a rich prayer life! This attitude enabled David to encourage himself (see 1 Sam. 30:6) when he was down. This is a habit we ought to develop and do on a regular basis; it's why the Bible makes specific mention of David doing so.

I want you to know that you don't have to enter into or leave your time with God depressed, sad, frustrated or annoyed. You can walk away from your prayer time with a smile on your face. You can walk away from your prayer time with His peace in your mind and in your heart. You can walk away from your prayer time full of joy because of your covenant relationship. Remember, God is on your side. He is your rock. He is your deliverer. He is your salvation.

Notice how David ends this psalm: "The LORD liveth; and blessed be my rock; and let the God of my salvation be exalted. It is God that avengeth me, and subdueth the people under me. He delivereth me from mine enemies: yea, thou liftest me up above those that rise up against me: thou hast delivered me from the violent man. Therefore will I give thanks unto thee, O LORD, among the heathen, and sing praises unto thy name. Great deliverance giveth he to his king; and sheweth mercy to his anointed, to David, and to his seed for evermore" (Ps. 18:46-50).

David ended this prayer the right way—with thanksgiving.

Be Thankful by Remembering What God Has Done

Psalm 103:2 tells us, "Praise the LORD, O my soul, and forget not all his benefits" (NIV). One of the best ways you can clothe yourself with a spirit of thanksgiving is by meditating on the psalms. I know it has benefited my own prayer life. I can't help but thank God when I read through the psalmists' powerful and beautiful writings on the nature and character of my great and mighty God. Here are a few of my favorite passages:

Hear, O LORD, and have mercy upon me: LORD, be thou my helper. Thou hast turned for me my mourning into dancing: thou hast put off my sackcloth, and girded me with gladness; to the end that my glory may sing praise to thee, and not be silent. O LORD my God, I will give thanks unto thee for ever (Ps. 30:10-12).

O give thanks unto the LORD; call upon his name: make known his deeds among the people. Sing unto him, sing psalms unto him: talk ye of all his wondrous works. Glory ye in his holy name: let the heart of them rejoice that seek the LORD. Seek the LORD, and his strength: seek his face evermore. Remember his marvellous works that he hath done; his wonders, and the judgments of his mouth (Ps. 105:1-5).

The words of these psalms are a wonderful way to start the Prayer of Petition—by talking about the wonderful works of God. You increase your faith when you do this. You build up your confidence. You embolden your prayers with the power of the Holy Spirit.

The early Church also knew the power in declaring the awesomeness of God when making their petitions. Their prayers in Acts 4:24-31 not only state their petitions, but they also show us how they filled them with praise from beginning to end.

There is an old song I used to sing while growing up that I still love hearing today. It's simple, and some of you may think it's a little old-fashioned, but there is great meaning behind it. Maybe you've heard of it?

Count your blessings, name them one by one.
Count your blessings, see what God has done.

Do you count your blessings on a regular basis? Do you thank God for the many great things He has already done in your life? When facing an impossible-looking situation, instead of going to God with a troubled mind and a troubled heart, and wondering if there is any way out of your circumstance, count your blessings. Start naming them to God one by one.

The next time you sit down and pray your Prayer of Petition and supplication, take a moment to remember the goodness and faithfulness of God. Remember how you have been delivered in times past. Remember how God has provided for you in times past. Remember some of the miracles He has performed in your life. Thank Him for all of these things.

Tell Him how thankful you are that He has made you into a new person. Tell Him how thankful you are that He filled you with the Holy Spirit. Tell Him how thankful you are that He restored your marriage, that He healed your babies, that He gave you good health. Tell Him how thankful you are that He has prospered you, and that He has put you in the center of His will.

Let me share with you some of the things I tell God I am thankful for before I begin my Prayer of Petition. I tell Him how grateful I am for my wife and for our daughters and grandchildren. I tell Him how grateful I am that He delivered me from a life of failure and changed me into a winner. I tell Him how grateful I am that He's allowed me to travel all over the world preaching the gospel. I tell Him how grateful I am that He has blessed my ministry. I tell Him how grateful I am that He has given me people who have confidence in me and want to hear what I have to say.

Friend, don't leave praise out of your prayer life. If you do, your Prayer of Petition and supplication will not be the same.

I want to share with you one more psalm. It's one of my favorites; and many times I pray this passage before I make my petition. It's one of the most faith-building Scriptures, because every verse is full of thanksgiving. It may be a little long to read, but it's so powerful. The next time you pray a petition, I want to encourage you to use it in your prayer.

Psalm 136

O give thanks unto the LORD; for he is good: for his mercy endureth for ever.

O give thanks unto the God of gods: for his mercy endureth for ever.

O give thanks to the Lord of lords: for his mercy endureth for ever.

To him who alone doeth great wonders: for his mercy endureth for ever.

To him that by wisdom made the heavens: for his mercy endureth for ever.

To him that stretched out the earth above the waters: for his mercy endureth for ever.

To him that made great lights: for his mercy endureth for ever:

The sun to rule by day: for his mercy endureth for ever:

The moon and stars to rule by night: for his mercy endureth for ever.

To him that smote Egypt in their firstborn: for his mercy endureth for ever:

And brought out Israel from among them: for his mercy endureth for ever:

With a strong hand, and with a stretched out arm: for his
   mercy endureth for ever.
To him which divided the Red sea into parts: for his mercy en-
   dureth for ever:
And made Israel to pass through the midst of it: for his mercy
   endureth for ever:
But overthrew Pharaoh and his host in the Red sea: for his
   mercy endureth for ever.
To him which led his people through the wilderness: for his
   mercy endureth for ever.
To him which smote great kings: for his mercy endureth for ever:
And slew famous kings: for his mercy endureth for ever:
Sihon king of the Amorites: for his mercy endureth for ever:
And Og the king of Bashan: for his mercy endureth for ever:
And gave their land for an heritage: for his mercy endureth
   for ever:
Even an heritage unto Israel his servant: for his mercy en-
   dureth for ever.
Who remembered us in our low estate: for his mercy endureth
   for ever:
And hath redeemed us from our enemies: for his mercy en-
   dureth for ever.
Who giveth food to all flesh: for his mercy endureth for ever.
O give thanks unto the God of heaven: for his mercy endureth
   for ever.

The writer of this psalm did an awesome thing. He made a record
of the wonderful things that God had done for His people from the

beginning of time, as recorded in Genesis, right up to his day. And after every divine miracle and provision that he wrote down, he concluded that particular thought with these words, "O give thanks . . . for his mercy endures forever" (v. 26).

When I finish quoting this psalm during my prayer time, I pick up right where the writer left off. I say, "Thank You, God, for delivering Jerry Savelle out of the miry pit . . . for Your mercy endures forever. Thank You, God, for saving my soul . . . for Your mercy endures forever. Thank You, God, for healing my body . . . for Your mercy endures forever." I don't stop there. I continue verbalizing my gratitude for what He has done in my life. Eventually I find myself getting so encouraged in my spirit that by the time I get to my petition, I have full confidence that the Lord will hear my prayer.

There's one more thing I want to mention, and it's a critical element. You can't have an attitude of gratitude without humility. The Prayer of Petition and supplication has nothing to do with barging into God's throne room and telling Him, "I'm Your child and You owe me, so answer my prayer."

It's a humbling thing to remember what God has done in your life. Humility removes ego or a self-serving attitude from your prayers. My confidence to come boldly before God's throne has nothing to do with me or who I am in the natural. All my confidence is drawn from who He is, what He has promised in His Word and what He has done in my life.

He has made me righteous. He has seated me in heavenly places with Him. He has made me a new creature. He has made me more than a conqueror. He has given me a future and a hope. He has surrounded me with His favor. I'm aware of these truths every day of my life, and I'm continually grateful for them.

It's a humbling thing to know that God will take the time to hear your prayer. Remember the words of Peter: "For God resisteth the proud, and giveth grace to the humble. Humble yourselves therefore under the mighty hand of God, that he may exalt you in due time" (1 Pet. 5:5-6).

Friend, before you move on to the next chapter, put this book down and take a few minutes to think of everything you can be thankful for. Has God worked in your life and proved His faithfulness? Has God provided for you? Has God given you a miracle? Has God moved a mountain out of your way? Don't you get excited just thinking about all the wonderful things He has done for you?

Give God the praise. Give God the glory. Give God thanksgiving. He deserves it, and your thanksgiving will birth in you a bold confidence that He will not only hear your petition, but He will also fulfill it.

CHAPTER 6

Stop Worrying

When you begin to create your Prayer of Petition, it's like going on a treasure hunt to find out what God's will is in your particular situation. Your petition could be for healing from a terminal illness, for your marriage to work, for your financial situation to improve, for your kids to return to the Lord, for your business to turn around. Whatever impossible-looking situation you are facing today, just know the Prayer of Petition is your channel to bring about the quickest results based on God's will.

One of the biggest temptations you will face after you have constructed your petition and presented it to God is worry. You may be tempted to think, *What if what I'm praying for won't come to pass? What if God doesn't hear me? What if my situation gets worse? What if others think I'm crazy to pray this way?* When you find yourself plagued by worry, there is a passage of Scripture, which I mentioned in the first chapter, that will help you:

> Therefore I say unto you, Take no thought for your life, what ye shall eat, or what ye shall drink; nor yet for your body, what ye shall put on. Is not the life more than meat, and the body than raiment? Behold the fowls of the air: for they sow not, neither do they reap, nor gather into barns; yet your heavenly Father feedeth them. Are ye not much better than they? (Matt. 6:25-26).

Remember Your Source

I want you to notice something in these verses. Who is taking care of the birds of the air? The Source is taking care of them.

I love getting up early and going for walks. One morning as I was working on this book, I took some time out and went for a walk near my house. As I was admiring God's creation and praying, I saw some of the most beautiful birds I have ever seen. They looked like little parakeets or canaries. There were about 25 of them gathered together, just chirping and pecking at the ground. They were all eating from a particular spot that had just been mowed. I remember thinking, *Wow! The Source is taking care of them.* Then I remembered verse 26: "Are ye not much better than they [the birds]?"

The next several verses read, "Which of you by taking thought can add one cubit unto his stature? And why take ye thought for raiment? Consider the lilies of the field, how they grow; they toil not, neither do they spin: And yet I say unto you, that even Solomon in all his glory was not arrayed like one of these. Wherefore, if God so clothe the grass of the field, which to day is, and to morrow is cast into the oven, shall he not much more clothe you, O ye of little faith?" (Matt. 6:27-30).

I love the last line Jesus said: "O ye of little faith." I want you to know that God responds to faith, and wherever He finds it, He is drawn to it. Second Chronicles 16:9 tells us that "the eyes of the LORD run to and fro throughout the whole earth, to shew himself strong in the behalf of them whose heart is perfect." One of the meanings for the word "perfect" in this passage is a heart that has faith. God's eyes scan the earth looking for someone who believes. I'd hate to think that He looked at my house and moved right past it because He couldn't find what He was looking for. When God sees your faith, you will find yourself in the right position to see Him move. You will see manifestations of His ability to be the source of your supply.

Therefore take no thought, saying, What shall we eat? or, What shall we drink? or, Wherewithal shall we be clothed? (For after all these things do the Gentiles seek:) for your heavenly Father knoweth that ye have need of all these things. But seek ye first the kingdom of God, and his righteousness; and all these things shall be added unto you. Take therefore no thought for the morrow: for the morrow shall take thought for the things of itself. Sufficient unto the day is the evil thereof (Matt. 6:31-34).

You Don't Have to Take It

The theme that Jesus is teaching in Matthew 6 is not to worry about anything, because He is your Source. I want you to notice this sentence: "Take therefore no thought for the morrow: for the morrow shall take thought for the things of itself" (v. 34). Thoughts will come. It's inevitable. When you are praying the Prayer of Petition and asking God to do the impossible, I can promise you that you'll start thinking some crazy thoughts.

Is this going to work?

Will God come through for me?

What am I going to do if God doesn't answer my prayer?

Oh my goodness. I'm on the verge of losing everything.

My situation is hopeless.

Thoughts will come into your mind, but you don't have to let them stay there. This reminds me of a story Kenneth Hagin loved to tell. A woman came up to him one time and said, "Brother Hagin, please pray that I'll never have another negative thought." He looked at her and said, "Lady, if I could pray that for you, then I'd pray that for myself. I can't keep the negative thoughts from coming, but I don't have to allow them to dwell in my mind."

If you receive a thought that is contrary to God's promise of meeting your needs, then don't take it. Reject it. Cast it down. Don't accept it. Don't receive it. You are in control of your mind (see 2 Cor. 10:5). No one and nothing else is. Too many people go around saying, "The devil made me do it." Let me make it very clear: The devil can't make you do anything that you don't give him the authority to do.

If you think it's the devil putting thoughts in your mind, then don't take them. Give them back. Say out loud, "I don't take that thought. That's not my thought. I don't receive that thought." We are taught in Ephesians 6:16 to lift up our shield of faith to quench every fiery dart the devil throws our way. In other words, we're in charge here, not Satan.

Here is what's going to happen if you don't take control of that thought. If it gets in and stays in your mind, it's going to eventually drop down into your heart and then come out of your mouth. Before you know it, you will start talking about that once-harmless thought. And when you start talking about it, you are going to—as I call it— block your blessing with your own words. God wants to prove Himself to you as your Source. He wants to show you that He has unlimited power; but if you are saying things that are contrary to His Word, then you will block Him from performing His Word.

Worry does more than dampen your spirit and cause you unnecessary grief. It also has the power to strangle or choke. As a matter of fact, that is one of the meanings of the word from the literal Greek translation. "And the cares of this world, and the deceitfulness of riches, and the lusts of other things entering in, choke the word, and it becometh unfruitful" (Mark 4:19). One of the reasons why Satan wants you to worry is because he knows it chokes the Word. And when the Word has been choked, it is rendered unfruitful or inoperative.

The worst thing you can do while you are waiting for your Prayer of Petition to come to pass is to worry. The only way that you can prevent yourself from worrying is to replace worry with thinking thoughts that are produced by the Word of God.

Worry is a product of fear. The opposite of fear is faith. "Faith cometh by hearing, and hearing by the word of God" (Rom. 10:17). Keeping yourself from worrying is accomplished by spending quality time in the Word.

In my early days as a believer, when I was just learning how to trust God and walk by faith, there were many times when I couldn't sleep at night because I would worry about a million different things. I literally had to get up from where I was, grab my Bible, go into another room and read the Scriptures. Sometimes I had to do this for hours until I was able to shut my mind down. And there were even times when the moment I laid my head on the pillow, the same thoughts would try to overpower me again.

Guess what? I had to get back up, grab my Bible and start confessing the Word again. I had to get to the place where I established an attitude that either the devil was going to quit, or I was; and I was certainly not going to be the first one to give up. This takes time and practice. You have to train yourself to do this every time you pray your petition and find yourself worrying.

I am writing this book at a time when the economy is in a big mess. Many financial experts are saying it's the worst crisis since the

Great Depression. I know a lot of people who are continuing to believe God for financial stability, but they are bombarded with worry.

What if the economy doesn't recover?

What if I lose my job?

What if the market crumbles?

What if I can't sell my house?

What if I can't afford to buy another house?

These same thoughts might be consuming your mind, even this very minute as you read this book. You might be worried, fearful, afraid, full of anxiety and fretful because of everything that's happening around you. If so, run to the Word. Grab your Bible and start confessing the Scripture. Shut that worry down so you don't let it choke and strangle what God wants to do for you.

Some Christians get mad at other Christians who refuse to worry. Have you ever noticed that? Maybe you know exactly what I'm talking about. Maybe you have some family members who hate it when you talk the Word instead of worrying. It's almost like they want you to get down, because that's where they are. Some people think it's their call in life to keep you down. If they are worried, sad or depressed, they want you to share the same feelings. Misery sure does love company!

Some people can even mistake your confidence in God for pride, ego and arrogance. They may accuse you of acting like you are better than everyone else. I had this problem with some of my family. Some of my loved ones thought Carolyn and I were nuts because we trusted God for so much in our lives. But guess who they called when they were in trouble? Or when they needed prayer? Or when they needed money? They called us. It was like we were on their speed dial!

Maybe we are a little nuts, but we're nuts who are blessed! We've learned how to believe His Word and bring forth the impossible time and time again. I've come to realize that God is faithful. I can truthfully say that in over 40 years of working with Him, He has never let me down.

Let me tell you something: Believing God instead of worrying is not a matter of being better than anybody else. It's a matter of knowing what the Word says. That's why Paul prayed that we be filled with the knowledge of God (see Col. 1:9). When you receive revelation in the knowledge of your heavenly Father, it causes you to be optimistic, positive and bold.

Here are a few encouraging Scriptures that you can confess when you find yourself drenched with worry after you pray the Prayer of Petition.

The LORD is my strength and my shield; my heart trusted in him, and I am helped: therefore my heart greatly rejoiceth; and with my song will I praise him (Ps. 28:7).

My times are in Your hands; deliver me from the hands of my foes and those who pursue me and persecute me (Ps. 31:15, *AMP*).

The Lord preserves the faithful, and plentifully pays back him who deals haughtily (Ps. 31:23, *AMP*).

The LORD knoweth the days of the upright: and their inheritance shall be for ever (Ps. 37:18).

God is our refuge and strength, a very present help in trouble. Therefore will not we fear, though the earth be removed, and though the mountains be carried into the midst of the sea; though the waters thereof roar and be troubled, though the mountains shake with the swelling thereof (Ps. 46:1-3).

Do not fear, for I am with you; do not anxiously look about you, for I am your God. I will strengthen you, surely I will help you, surely I will uphold you with My righteous right hand (Isa. 41:10, *NASB*).

For I am the LORD, your God, who takes hold of your right hand and says to you, Do not fear; I will help you (Isa. 41:13, *NIV*).

The Lord is good, a Strength and Stronghold in the day of trouble; He knows (recognizes, has knowledge of, and understands) those who take refuge and trust in Him (Nah. 1:7, *AMP*).

Yet in all these things we are more than conquerors through Him who loved us. For I am persuaded that neither death nor life, nor angels nor principalities nor powers, nor things present nor things to come, nor height nor depth, nor any other created thing, shall be able to separate us from the love of God which is in Christ Jesus our Lord (Rom. 8:37-39, *NKJV*).

I called on the LORD in distress; the LORD answered me and set me in a broad place. The LORD is on my side; I will not fear. What can man do to me? The LORD is for me among those who help me; therefore I shall see my desire on those who hate me (Ps. 118:5-7, *NKJV*).

All these verses are comforting to me because they indicate that I don't have to spend all my prayer time trying to tell God what I'm going through. Many Christians don't truly understand this point. They think that prayer time means yelling, screaming, crying, bawling and squalling (as we say in Texas), trying to convince God that they are going through some pretty serious situations and need His help. But, folks, He already knows. The Bible tells us that God knows our days. He knows our time. There is nothing that He doesn't know.

You Are Always in God's Face

Psalm 41:12 says, "And as for me, thou upholdest me in mine integrity, and settest me before thy face for ever." Do you know what that means? It means my face is in God's face. And so is yours. Forever. That's why we never have to go before God and say, "Hey, God, do You remember me?"

I remember a situation years ago when Brother Kenneth Copeland and I were preaching in Omaha, Nebraska. This was when I first started out in the ministry and was working with him as his associate. I hadn't started teaching in his services yet. I was serving him and organizing and setting up the meetings. I was his staff. I was his road crew. Today he has more than 500 employees working for him, but back then it was pretty much me. I like to remind him all the time that when you lose a good man, it takes 500 to replace him!

During the services—which were three a day—I'd sit up on the platform with him. Many times I got so full and needed an outlet to share with someone else what I was learning. So in between services, in whatever city we were in, I went into the streets. I found drug addicts, prostitutes and alcoholics, and I would minister to them. Sometimes I would win to the Lord as many people in the streets as Brother Copeland did in the meetings.

After I led them to the Lord, I'd bring them to the meetings. Sometimes I had two or three front rows full of these new converts. We often had our meetings in nice hotel ballrooms, and these drunks would stagger in there and say with slurred speech, "Where's Jerry Savelle? Where's that meeting?" When Brother Copeland would look out at the audience and see the first few rows full of what someone would consider less-than-respectable-looking people, he would just shake his head and laugh. He'd say, "Jerry's been witnessing again. Look at the front row."

Well, in Omaha, there was one young man I met on the streets. I walked down the railroad tracks after him and followed him into a boxcar. When I got in that boxcar, there were about five others in there, and I started witnessing to all of them. I found myself being drawn to this one fellow. I asked him what his name was and he told me, "They call me California Shorty because I'm from California and I'm short."

"Well, California Shorty," I said, "I'm Jerry Savelle. God told me to follow you and to share the gospel with you because you don't have to live like this for the rest of your life." They all received what I said and invited Jesus into their lives. That night, I took all those men to Brother Copeland's meeting and sat them on the front row.

The subject that night was about prayer that brings results. I remember Brother Copeland saying, "Folks, what you need to learn to do is to talk to God like you'd talk to your best friend. Don't try to use Elizabethan English. That's for Elizabeth, not you." California Shorty liked what he was hearing and stood up and said, "Hey, Lord, this is California Shorty. Do you remember me?" The whole room burst into laughter.

Some time later, we were in another city and there were a lot of religious people there who didn't like what Brother Copeland was preaching. Out of the blue, California Shorty showed up. We didn't even know he was going to be there. As Brother Copeland preached and I sat behind him on the platform, enjoying the powerful service, I heard some noise out in the hallway. It was getting louder and louder and was beginning to disrupt the meeting. I had to go see what the commotion was about. I walked off the platform and headed toward the back door to do some investigating.

When I got back there, I saw a man lying on the floor begging for mercy. And California Shorty was right beside him. He had this poor guy by the collar and was about to hit him. He was saying, "Those are my preachers in there. Don't you ever talk ugly about Brother Copeland or Brother Jerry, or I'll whip you good." Even though I didn't fully support this tactic, I was tickled. I mean, it was pretty funny. I did, however, manage to get California Shorty off this guy and have him apologize to him.

I will never forget the question California Shorty asked in the first meeting he came to. "Lord, do you remember me?" It's been with me ever since. I'm always reminded of it because so many people don't think that God remembers them. I want to encourage you that He does remember you. He remembers you because you are always in His face. I want you to go to bed tonight knowing that you are in God's face. Cast your cares on Him. Stop worrying. Offer Him your Prayer of Petition and allow yourself to be built up in faith and have confidence that He has heard your prayer and will see you through.

Stop Worrying and Start Praying for Others

In whatever rough times you are going through right now where you need God's immediate intervention, be encouraged. God, the Source, is fully aware. Do you know how this knowledge can serve you? When you refuse to worry because you understand that God is your Source, and your times are in His hands, you can present Him your Prayer of Petition and then start praying for other people. You're so confident that He will answer your prayer that now you have the opportunity to pray for your friends, relatives, coworkers and others that the Lord puts on your heart.

Over the years, I've discovered that the sooner I get me and my needs off my mind and get involved in the needs of other people, I get one step closer to seeing God work in my behalf. First Thessalonians 4:12 tells us that if we "walk honestly toward them that are without . . . ye may have lack of nothing." In other words, if we receive the revelation that God is our Source, that He knows what we need, that our time is in His hands, we can use our time and energy in a more fruitful way by being a blessing to somebody else, interceding for somebody else and sowing into somebody else's life.

Since I've learned about the effectiveness and the power of the Prayer of Petition, I can tell you that I spend very little time praying for myself or my needs. Somebody asked me, "Brother Jerry, how many hours a day do you pray?" I said, "That's a good question. I really don't know." He continued, "But you've been in the ministry for 40 years. You must pray all day." While I am in prayer mode all the time, I don't focus a lot on myself.

In all my years of following God, He's never let me down once. So why should I start worrying now and spend all my time talking to Him about me when He's already proven that He takes care of Jerry Savelle? I think the best use of my time is to intercede for someone else, to look for an opportunity to be a blessing to somebody else and to help someone else enjoy victory.

I'm telling you today that one of the quickest ways to get your needs met is to get involved in meeting the needs of somebody else. There's just something about doing that that attracts God to you. I call that Christianity at another level.

Instead of worrying about your situation, be confident. Be assured. Rest in the revelation that God will provide for you. He will never let you down.

Sample Prayer of Petition for Freedom from Mental Anguish

Worry is a spiritual force that is tied in with many ailments and disorders, such as depression, anxiety and severe mood fluctuation. I know a lot of people who feel mentally and emotionally tormented, and they don't know how to obtain peace.

Maybe you can relate. Maybe you find it hard to sometimes even get out of bed in the morning. Maybe you can't remember the last time you smiled. Maybe you can't sleep at night because you are plagued by anxiety, worry or fear. Maybe you even feel suicidal.

I want to offer you hope today. Hope in the form of healing from your loving Creator. Your heavenly Father wants you to be healthy emotionally and mentally. This is part of living a blessed and abundant life.

If you are struggling today with some form of internal anguish, I offer you this special Prayer of Petition:

Be it known this day, _____, _____ (A.M./P.M.), that I receive the heavenly grant for my mental and emotional healing. Father, in the name of Jesus, I come boldly to the throne of grace and present Your Word.

According to John 16:23, Jesus said, "I assure you, most solemnly I tell you, that My Father will grant you whatever you ask in My Name" (AMP). In 1 Corinthians 2:16 it is written that we have the mind of Christ. The mind of Christ is not tormented by anxiety, worry or fear. The mind of Christ is full of the peace that passes understanding (see Phil. 4:7).

Psalm 147:3 tells me, "He heals the brokenhearted and binds up their wounds [curing their pains and their sorrows]" (AMP). I pray that You heal the brokenness in my heart and in my mind and that You bind up my wounds so that I may receive a mind that is renewed (see Eph. 4:3). Your Word tells me that "a bruised reed shall he not break, and the smoking flax shall he not quench" (Isa. 42:3). I believe it, Lord. And I believe that You will answer me and strengthen me in my inner self (see Ps. 138:3).

Father, I know and I thank You that whoever will put their trust in You will never be forsaken (see Ps. 9:10). I thank You that You have heard my petition. I thank You that You are my strength and shield, and because of that I rejoice. I will bless You because You have heard my supplication (see Ps. 28: 6-7).

I thank You today, Lord, that I am delivered and free of my mental and emotional torment. You have healed me. You have renewed my mind. You have renewed my spirit. And You have given me peace. Never again will I be bound by _____, but I will be covered with Your peace, Your joy and Your presence.

_____   _____

(Signature)   (Date)

CHAPTER 7

More than Confident

When you pray the will of God, you develop a confidence that the end result in the situation you are praying for will be favorable.

Be Confident in God

"And this is the confidence (the assurance, the privilege of boldness) which we have in Him: [we are sure] that if we ask anything (make any request) according to His will (in agreement with His own plan), He listens to and hears us. And if (since) we [positively] know that He listens to us in whatever we ask, we also know [with settled and absolute knowledge] that we have [granted us as our present possessions] the requests made of Him" (1 John 5:14-15, *AMP*). When you know that what you are asking for is in line with God's purpose, then you can't help but experience a confidence that your prayer will come to pass.

How does this confidence come about? And why don't more Christians have it? I know for a fact that many lack confidence in their prayers because if they prayed with the kind of confidence John talked about, they wouldn't need to be in every prayer line that is formed when they attend church services. They wouldn't be calling the pastor every night asking for his prayers.

Our organization gets a lot of prayer requests. They keep coming in, more and more with each passing day. This tells me that there are a lot of people with a lot of needs and who are not very confident in their own prayer life. Don't misunderstand me, we love praying for people, but some of them by now should know how to pray with confidence themselves.

Every Christian ought to have confidence in their prayer life. I remember when our daughters were young. Even as little girls, we taught them to believe in God and to pray. I used to sit them on the couch, put a Bible in their laps and preach to them as if they could understand every single word I was saying. Most times, they ended up falling asleep, but that was okay. I was instilling the Word of God in them.

Our girls had great confidence, especially in the prayers of their mommy and daddy. Every time Jerriann would hurt herself, she would run over to me and say, "Daddy, pray it." She believed that if Daddy prayed it, it would work. She would feel better. Her pain would go away. It didn't matter how badly she was hurting or how hard she was crying; she knew deep down in her heart that somehow if Daddy prayed then it would get better.

This is confidence. She had confidence in my prayers. Think about this. How much more fulfilling and enriching our prayer lives would be if we shared that same feeling of confidence in our heavenly Father!

I know that confidence doesn't happen overnight, but you have to start developing it one night. There comes a point in everyone's life when you have to start building a strong confidence in God's ability to hear you and come through for you.

You need to know that God hears your prayers. Your confidence should not be found only in the prayers of your pastor, your spouse, your best friend or a preacher on TV. Your confidence should be found in what God can do in and for you because of your own prayer that is based on His Word. At some point, you have to stop being the one who always needs to be prayed for and start being the one who prays for others. The more you study the Word, the more confidence you will have. Confidence doesn't have anything to do with how eloquently you pray; it has everything to do with God being who He is. Your confidence comes from Him and Him alone.

The Grantor of Desires

When you pray the Prayer of Petition and end your prayer with the "Amen," that really means, "So be it." When I offer God my Prayer of Petition, I want to walk away from that prayer time with my head held up high and a smile on my face, confident in my heart that I know God heard me, and it's just a matter of time before He intervenes.

Psalm 20:1-4 says, "May the Lord answer you in the day of trouble! May the name of the God of Jacob set you up on high [and defend you]; send you help from the sanctuary and support, refresh, and strengthen you from Zion; remember all your offerings and accept your burnt sacrifice. Selah [pause, and think of that]! May He grant you according to your heart's desire and fulfill all your plans" (*AMP*). These are some faith-building verses! They were inspired by God. The Holy Spirit inspired David to pray that the Lord would hear us in the time of trouble. God doesn't contradict Himself. He wouldn't tell someone to write something down that wasn't true. David also tells us in verse 4 that God will "grant you according to your heart's desire and fulfill all your plans." That's an interesting statement.

When I first came to the Lord, a few people in my life told me that God *might* meet my needs, but you just never knew. There were folks who also told me that God was not interested in any of my desires or wants. They suggested that I never even mention anything to God about something I wanted. I was told not to let my hopes get too high because "you just never know what God might do."

When I read Psalm 20, however, I don't find any truth in what these people were telling me. This passage, God-inspired Scripture, tells me that God will not only meet my needs, but He wants to give me my heart's desires. Psalm 37:4 says the same thing: "Delight thyself also in the LORD: and he shall give thee the desires of thine heart."

I want to share with you about a Prayer of Petition I wrote where God gave me my heart's desires. I pray that this will build up your confidence that God can do the same thing for you. In 1972, the Full Gospel Businessmen's organization was holding its world convention in Honolulu, Hawaii. My wife and I wanted to go and be in that meeting. One night before we went to bed, my wife told me that she, too, felt we were supposed to be there. So we began to believe God for it.

At that time, we were believing God for everything. We were believing God for food on our table. We were believing God for food for our babies. We were believing God for clothes on our back. We were believing God for gas so I could drive to work every day. And here we were, talking about a trip to Hawaii. What a crazy idea! In the natural, it seemed impossible. But I dared to believe that God could grant this desire.

I told Carolyn I was going to write out a Prayer of Petition and ask God to give us the money needed to get to that conference in Hawaii. She was excited. "Absolutely!" she told me. "You do the research, you write out the prayer and then we'll read and pray it together out loud." I got to work on my prayer.

First, I had to figure out how much the trip would cost. Second, I researched the price of airfare, hotel, the conference and the amount we would need to get a baby-sitter to watch our girls. Then I spent a lot of time researching the Word of God and finding Scripture about

God giving us the desires of our heart. I used Psalm 20 as the foundation of my prayer. Once I got all the Scripture together, I wrote out my Prayer of Petition and made two copies, one for my wife and one for myself. I still have my copy today. Here's what we prayed:

Be it known this day of May the 15th, 1972, 11:25 P.M., just before midnight. I believe I receive a heavenly grant in the amount of $900. Father, in the name of Jesus, I come boldly to the throne of grace and I present You Your Word. And according to John 16:23, Jesus, You said, "I assure you, most solemnly, I tell you, that My Father will grant you whatever you ask in My Name" (AMP). Jesus, You said in Mark 11:24, "Whatever you ask for in prayer, believe (trust and be confident) that it is granted to you, and you will [get it]" (AMP).

Father, in Luke 6:38 You said, "Give, and it shall be given unto you; good measure, pressed down, and shaken together, and running over, shall men give unto your bosom." And in accordance to Your Word, I sow. I give in order to set the spiritual law of giving and receiving, sowing and reaping, to work in my behalf.

And, Father, in accordance with Matthew 18:18, I bind Satan and all his forces. I render them helpless and unable to operate. They will not hinder my grant. I loose the ministering spirits according to Hebrews 1, verses 13 and 14. You said they have been sent to minister unto them who are heirs of salvation. And I charge them to go forth and cause my grant to come into my hands. The amount of this grant, $900, will cover airfare, food, lodging, expenses and baby-sitting wages for my children. Jesus, You said in Matthew 18:19, "Again I say unto you, that if two of you shall agree . . ." and, Lord, my wife and I are in agreement. We believe that You will grant whatever we have asked.

Therefore, we say in Jesus' name we believe, we receive now; and as a point of contact to release our faith, we sign our names to this petition.

By the way, you might be laughing right now because we asked for only $900. It may seem like chump change to some of you today. Let me tell you something: In 1972, $900 was a lot of money. There was no way I could have come up with that on my own. The night my wife and I prayed this petition, we went to sleep with a smile on our faces. There was less than a month left before the conference.

The day before the trip, I had $750. We still needed $150. We had no idea where we were going to come up with that difference, but Carolyn and I believed. The Bible says that faith demands action, so I told my wife, "Carolyn, pack your bags." We got our suitcases ready the night before we were supposed to leave and put them in the living room.

A few hours later, we heard a knock on the door. A man stood outside and told us, "I heard you two are going to Hawaii. My wife and I want to sow into that trip." He gave us $200. Carolyn and I rejoiced and spent the rest of the evening thanking and praising God. My mother offered to come and watch our girls, and she didn't want us to pay her anything. God not only met our need and fulfilled our desire, but He also provided more than enough.

Friend, I want to help you build up your confidence. I want you to know that God is a God who does exceedingly, abundantly and above all you can ask or think. Not only will He take care of your needs, but He will also give you the desires of your heart. As you invest your time and energy into constructing and praying your Prayer of Petition, I pray that your faith will increase and your confidence will become stronger as you believe God to do what you once thought was impossible.

Confidence-Building Scripture

As you know, I love to use the psalms for many reasons in the Prayer of Petition and supplication. I want to give you a couple of confidence-building passages that you can meditate on when you are praying your petition. As you read this book, it's also helpful to highlight the passages I've talked about (and will continue to explore) and continually look at them whenever you feel discouraged.

"Let my supplication come before You; deliver me according to Your word" (Ps. 119:170, *NKJV*). In this text, the psalmist is basing his supplication on what he found out God's Word said about his situation.

Here is another passage that I love:

Unto you do I cry, O Lord my Rock, be not deaf and silent to me, lest, if You be silent to me, I become like those going down to the pit [the grave].

Hear the voice of my supplication as I cry to You for help, as I lift up my hands toward Your innermost sanctuary (the Holy of Holies).

Drag me not away with the wicked, with the workers of iniquity, who speak peace with their neighbors, but malice and mischief are in their hearts.

Repay them according to their work and according to the wickedness of their doings; repay them according to the work of their hands; render to them what they deserve.

Because they regard not the works of the Lord nor the operations of His hands, He will break them down and not rebuild them.

Blessed be the Lord, because He has heard the voice of my supplications.

The Lord is my Strength and my [impenetrable] Shield; my heart trusts in, relies on, and confidently leans on Him, and I am helped; therefore my heart greatly rejoices, and with my song will I praise Him.

The Lord is their [unyielding] Strength, and He is the Stronghold of salvation to [me] His anointed.

Save Your people and bless Your heritage; nourish and shepherd them and carry them forever (Ps. 28:1-9, *AMP*).

Notice verse 2 reads, "Hear my supplication." And in verse 6 it says, "Blessed be the Lord because he hath heard my supplications." The writer is assured that God has heard his prayer. I like this psalm because it demonstrates a connection between prayer and confidence.

As a matter of fact, this is true throughout the Bible. Usually, when you see the word "petition" or "supplication" in the Word of God, you are going to find a reference to confidence connected to it. Why? Because whenever you pray something according to what you have discovered is the known will of God, you can be assured it will come to pass.

It's just like knowing someone's intentions and motivations and having faith that what they say they will do, they will do. Do you have a friend, coworker, ministry partner or family member that you know always has your best interests in mind, and you know that you can count on them for anything? If you need them to do something for you, you can trust them to come through for you when you need it, right?

Well, how much more confident can you be in depending on God and on His infallible and unchanging Word? His intentions for our lives only benefit us. "For I know the thoughts that I think toward you, saith the LORD, thoughts of peace, and not of evil, to give you an expected end" (Jer. 29:11). Rest in the confidence that the Prayer of Petition based on the known will of God will be heard.

When Doubt Creeps In

Just as you may find yourself caught in worry after you pray your petition, sometimes doubt can stand in the way of confidence. Many people tend to doubt God's willingness. Most of us don't have any trouble believing that God *can* heal our body, *can* get us out of debt, *can* repair our marriage, *can* deliver us from addiction or *can* provide for our children, yet we have trouble believing God's willingness to do those things for us. Do you want to know something? Sometimes I think it's more insulting to doubt that God *wants* to do something for you than it is for you to doubt that He *can* do something for you.

When we doubt God's willingness, we doubt His love for us. The Bible says that God is love, so if we doubt His love, then we doubt the validity of His Word. My friend, I assure you, God's Word is true.

God loves and cares for you. When you pray the Prayer of Petition, be confident that He knows your need. Be confident that He hears your cries. Be confident that He cares. Be confident that He is going to come through for you. Be saturated with confidence from that knowledge. Let it sink deep into your heart and help you withstand the pressures that can come from seemingly impossible situations. Rest in that confidence.

You can be confident in your prayer because you are praying His will. Don't allow doubt to settle in your heart and make you start thinking God doesn't want to step in and intervene on your behalf. His will is for you to be at peace, to be healthy, to be prosperous and to be successful. That is what brings God delight. Psalm 35:27 says, "Let them shout for joy, and be glad, that favour my righteous cause: yea, let them say continually, Let the LORD be magnified, which hath pleasure in the prosperity of his servant."

I want to share with you a testimony from my daughter Terri about how she applied the Prayer of Petition in her own life and how she chose to be confident in God in what seemed to be an impossible-looking situation in her life.

After Terri lost a baby through miscarriage, there was a long period of time when she wasn't able to conceive. She was believing God for a baby, but nothing was happening. Something was wrong, but the doctors couldn't figure out what the problem was. Terri and I were talking one day, and I encouraged her to write a Prayer of Petition for the baby she and my son-in-law Rodney desired.

She started gathering her facts. She knew that it was God's will for her to be fruitful and multiply. She also knew that it was God's will to give her the desires of her heart. She started working on her Prayer of Petition and wrote out that she wanted a little girl with "red hair who had long legs like her daddy and was smart like her mother." (That's how she always told this story.) She was very specific in her particulars. She even wrote down that she wanted the baby to be born in February.

After she researched it, wrote it and prayed it, Terri started sowing seed. She hosted more baby showers than she had ever been to in her whole life. And she kept believing. Let me tell you, it wasn't always easy. The devil kept whispering to her, "You'll never have a baby. Everyone around you will get pregnant, but you won't." But my daughter threw aside those doubts and kept her confidence in God's Word and His will for her life. She trusted that whatever was written in His Word was the final authority. Not the devil. Not those around her. Not the doctors. Not even her body.

I want you to know that everything came to pass exactly as Terri wrote down. My granddaughter, Kassidi Cherie, is a beautiful redhead. She even has legs like her daddy and is just as smart as her mommy!

Notice that Terri didn't just pray, "God, if it be Your will, let me have a child." That wouldn't create any confidence in her spirit. That kind of prayer would easily discourage anyone. She had to pray with confidence based on the Word of God. That is what made her faith unshakeable. That is what made her able to stand in front of the devil and say, "No, Satan. You are wrong. It is written . . ."

Terri tells me she always keeps that petition with her. It reminds her that she is a winner and the devil is a loser. It reminds her that God is more powerful than any need that may arise in her life. It reminds her that God's Word is the final authority and she can rest knowing He will take care of her.

Along with the confidence that comes from praying the will of God, you can also expect God's peace to come into your life. We'll talk about this more in the following chapter. But let me encourage you once more to come to the place in your life where you are confident and fully persuaded that God not only hears your prayers but that He also fulfills them. His Word promises this; now dare to believe it.

CHAPTER 8

Make Room for Peace

The apostle Paul wrote, "Be careful for nothing; but in every thing by prayer and supplication with thanksgiving let your requests be made known unto God. And the peace of God, which passeth all understanding, shall keep your hearts and minds through Christ Jesus" (Phil. 4:6-7).

Take note of when Paul is saying this peace of God will come. Think about what goes on when you are wrestling with a particular situation or have a need that can only be taken care of with divine providence. Think about your Prayer of Petition. When is peace of greatest importance? The moment you pray—the moment all your requests and desires about that situation come out of your mouth and you call upon God to intervene.

The devil will start his attack the moment you take that first step of faith and go into prayer. That's when you are going to need peace the most, because he will begin harping on you in an instant. You know it's true.

How many times have you prayed in the past and found yourself barely able to get past the Amen, before the devil is whispering negative thoughts and doubts in your ear? This happens to all of us. The devil says things like, "It won't work." "Who do you think you are to ask for this?" "God is much too busy to hear your little prayer."

You need the peace of God when you first utter your Prayer of Petition and the devil throws his best shot at you and tries with all his might to discourage you and tells you lies to keep you from believing that God can do all things. That's the moment when you need the peace of God that goes beyond our understanding, to guard your heart and mind.

I like reading Philippians 4:6-7 in the *Amplified Bible*: "Do not fret or have any anxiety about anything, but in every circumstance and in everything, by prayer and petition (definite requests) with thanksgiving, continue to make your wants known to God. And God's peace [shall be yours, that tranquil state of a soul assured of its salvation through Christ, and so fearing nothing from God and being content with its earthly lot of whatever sort that is, that peace] which transcends all understanding shall garrison and mount guard over your hearts and minds in Christ Jesus."

Now that's some powerful stuff. When you pray the Prayer of Petition and supplication with thanksgiving and confidence, you can count on the peace that passes all understanding to come and quiet your heart and mind.

What's on Your Mind?

Right after Paul encouraged us by saying how prayer and God's peace go hand in hand, he gave us another admonishment: "Finally, brethren, whatsoever things are true, whatsoever things are honest, whatsoever things are just, whatsoever things are pure, whatsoever things are lovely, whatsoever things are of good report; if there be any virtue, and if there be any praise, think on these things. Those things, which ye have both learned, and received, and heard, and seen in me, do: and the God of peace shall be with you" (Phil. 4:8-9).

Keep in mind that Paul didn't change subjects in between verses 7 and 8. When he talked about prayer and the peace of God, and instructed us to think about good things, these two ideas are connected. It's important to note that the moment you pray and expect the peace of God to saturate your mind, you have to become very selective about what you think about afterwards.

The greatest battles you will ever fight are in your mind. You can actually destroy the power of your prayer simply by what you think about. You must not allow your mind to run wild and think whatever it wants to think. You have the ability to keep it under control and allow the Word of God to dominate your thought life.

This is what Paul was referring to when he wrote, "But clothe yourself with the Lord Jesus Christ (the Messiah), and make no provision for [indulging] the flesh [put a stop to thinking about the evil cravings of your physical nature] to [gratify its] desires (lusts)" (Rom. 13:14, *AMP*). The way you make "provision for the flesh" is by thinking the wrong thoughts. When you think negatively, you are indulging the flesh.

A New Way to Look at Sowing and Reaping

The fact is, what you think about the most is the direction your life is going to go. Negative thoughts will cause your life to go in a negative direction; positive thoughts will cause your life to go in a positive direction. If you think depressing or oppressing thoughts all the time, you are going to end up the most depressed and oppressed person in your neighborhood.

Galatians 6:7 reads, "Be not deceived; God is not mocked: for whatsoever a man soweth, that shall he also reap." This familiar verse tells us that we determine our own happiness or misery based upon the seeds that we sow. So the key to living a totally successful life, and the key to successfully praying the Prayer of Petition, lies in the proper application of this law. In the natural, the spiritual law of sowing and reaping is commonly referred to as the law of cause and effect.

While there are many kinds of seeds we can sow concerning our finances, our time or even kindness, the seeds I am specifically talking about in this chapter are thoughts, ideas and concepts. There are both positive seeds and negative seeds, and you and I stand in a very strategic place. We are the only ones who possess the authority to determine which type of seeds (thoughts, ideas and concepts) we will sow into our own lives. I determine what kind of seed I sow, and you determine what kind of seed you sow.

The fact is, your mind is a battleground. It is the place that God must fill with His peace. But this can only happen if the seed that's in it is good seed. Good seed is what makes room for God's peace to saturate your heart.

I want to be clear about something: If you don't like the way you are living right now, it's not somebody else's fault. It's your responsibility. If your life is one of happiness, it's because you have sown seeds of happiness. If your life is one of misery, it's because you have sown seeds of negativity. You can blame abuse from your childhood. You can blame the man or woman who hurt you yesterday or some time in your past. You can blame a tragedy you experienced or a period of time when you were really sick. You can point to any number of things or people and say it's that thing or that person's fault for the poor condition of your life; but that's not what the Bible says.

This passage in Galatians is clear. A man or woman's harvest in life depends entirely upon the seeds that he or she sows. So, to properly apply this spiritual law of sowing and reaping, you have to take responsibility for your life. You have to take responsibility for your life's outcome. Specifically, you have to take responsibility for your thought life.

If you pray the Prayer of Petition and constantly dwell on thoughts like these—*God will never hear my prayer; My need is too great; This is a waste of time; I don't know how God can come through for me*—guess what will happen? Exactly what you are thinking. *What you sow, you will reap*, especially in the Prayer of Petition.

I learned some new things about this spiritual law when I was preaching with Brother Kenneth Copeland and his wife, Gloria, in England, back in November 1992. In the opening service, Brother Copeland was teaching out of the book of Genesis. While he was reading a particular passage of Scripture, the Spirit of God asked me a question that really didn't have anything to do with what Brother Copeland was talking about.

God said, "When I first created man, what was the first gift I bestowed upon him?" I knew the answer to that and I immediately responded with, "Authority and dominion." I knew that because that is what Genesis 1:26 tells us.

Then He asked me, "What was the second gift I gave to man?" First of all, I have never looked at what God gave Adam as "gifts," so I found that very interesting. I had no idea what the second gift was! I said, "God, I don't know what gift number two was." He replied, "Well, if gift number one was found (starting) in Genesis 1:26, read what follows those verses and tell me the answer." I did, and here is what I found:

And God said, Behold, I have given you every herb bearing seed, which is upon the face of all the earth, and every tree, in which is the fruit of a tree yielding seed; to you it shall be for meat (Gen. 1:29).

Notice what the second gift was—seed. God gave mankind the gift of authority first and seed second. Do know what this tells us? It tells us that from the beginning of time, God has given you and me the authority to determine our own outcome based upon the seeds that we sow.

Thoughts are seeds. If a thought is a negative thought, it will grow and affect your life in a negative way. If that seed is a positive seed, it will grow and affect your life in a positive way.

The problem I see so often with most people is that they have dwelt for years on negative thoughts, ideas and concepts, and the result is that they live lives of misery. They see other people living better lives and they want to live that way, but they haven't discovered or are not willing to apply this life-changing principle of sowing and reaping.

Your mind is like a computer. It has to be programmed. You are programming it either with negative thoughts, ideas and concepts or with positive thoughts, ideas and concepts. When you pray the Prayer of Petition, you have to partner with God by giving Him a mind that is full of good seed.

Instead of thinking, *My prayer will never work,* think, *I believe God will answer my petition.* Instead of thinking, *This is too hard for God,* think, *Nothing is impossible with God.* Instead of thinking, *What I am praying for is too big for God to handle,* think, *I know that God can intervene and will fulfill His Word and His will in my life.*

How do we know we can do this? Because Paul, by the Holy Spirit, instructed us in 2 Corinthians 10:3-5 that we have mighty weapons available to us and that we are to cast down every thought that exalts itself against what God's Word says. And God wouldn't tell us to do something that we can't do.

I want to show you a scriptural example of how this law works in the negative and in the positive. Here's the negative. Job said, "Even as I have seen, they that plow iniquity, and sow wickedness, reap the same" (Job 4:8). *THE MESSAGE* puts it this way: "It's my observation that those who plow evil and sow trouble reap evil and trouble." Here's the positive side: "Sow to yourselves in righteousness, reap in mercy; break up your fallow ground: for it is time to seek the LORD, till he come and rain righteousness upon you" (Hos. 10:12).

You can sow in the negative and reap negative, or you can sow in the positive and reap positive. I feel confident that you want positive things to happen. And I'm confident that you want your Prayer of Petition to come to pass. Sow good seed!

You get in life exactly what you sow, and it all begins with a thought, an idea and a concept. The same applies to the Prayer of Petition. If you sow into your prayer thoughts that are fixed on God and on His Word, believing that He can do all things in your behalf, then you will reap a harvest of peace and a fulfilled Prayer of Petition.

The most successful people in the world are those who have trained their minds to perceive what is possible even when it looks impossible. They look beyond the obstacle that is blocking their success and recognize that through perseverance and by remaining positive in their thinking they will ultimately be victorious. When you pray the Prayer of Petition, you are praying about something that looks impossible in the natural.

Sow good seed into your prayer and dare to believe. Sow good seed into your prayer and have faith in God's ability to answer it.

Sow good seed into your prayer and cast aside all negative thoughts.

Scripture teaches us to "look not at the things which are seen, but at the things which are not seen: for the things which are seen are temporal; but the things which are not seen are eternal" (2 Cor. 4:18). The word "temporal" means temporary. I love the definition the Lord gave me way back in the early 1970s. He said "temporal" means "subject to change."

If you can see it, then your situation is subject to change. If you believe God's Word more than what your situation is telling you, then your situation is subject to change. If you pray the Prayer of Petition in faith and keep thinking right thoughts, then your seemingly impossible situation is subject to change.

Paul admonished us to think about things that are true, honest, just, pure, lovely, things that have a good report (see Phil. 4:8-9). In others words, you have to be very selective about what you allow to get into your mind. You have a choice as to what seed you sow. Sometimes this means paying no mind to people around you who only focus on the negative. And it might even mean not hanging around these kinds of folk.

You don't have to sit around and listen to Mr. Doom and Gloom drone on and on about something bad that is designed to discourage you. You don't have to sit around and listen to Ms. Pity-Party talk about how life stinks. You can get to the place where, as negative people talk about negative things, you can put a smile on your face, turn a deaf ear to what they are saying and think on something good while they are talking all their bad.

Sow good seed!

Don't Limit God with Bad Seed

God is unlimited, but we can put limitations on Him. And when we do, we prevent Him from working in our lives. Psalm 78:41 says, "Yea, they turned back and tempted God, and limited the Holy One of Israel."

God wants you to pray the Prayer of Petition, and He wants to respond to that prayer and make the impossible possible. But if you dwell on things that are negative, or if you fail to fight the battle in your mind, or if you speak words of discouragement, doubt and fear, then you will block what He wants to do for you—and that includes answering your Prayer of Petition (see Matt. 14:31; 17:17; Mark 9:22-24).

I want to show you where limitations come from and how you can overcome them. "A good man out of the good treasure of the heart brings forth good things, and an evil man out of the evil treasure brings forth evil things" (Matt. 12:35, *NKJV*). Instead of the phrase "brings forth," the *Amplified Bible* uses the phrase "flings forth." Notice that this verse can operate both in the positive and in the negative. An evil man, out of the evil treasure of his heart, flings out evil things; and a good man, out of the good treasures of his heart, flings out good things.

In both cases, these people are getting results. The negative man is getting negative results; the positive man is getting positive results. What's the difference? The good man thinks on positive ideas, thoughts and concepts; when they drop down into his spirit, these ideas, thoughts and concepts come out of his spirit and become reality. On the other hand, the evil man constantly dwells on negative thoughts, ideas and concepts. They drop down into his spirit, and out of his spirit negative ideas, thoughts and concepts become reality.

So where do limitations come from? Limitations come from negative seed, or from the negative thoughts we allow into our minds and then drop down into our hearts. Let's look at 2 Corinthians 10:1-5 again:

> Now I Paul myself beseech you by the meekness and gentleness of Christ, who in presence am base among you, but being absent am bold toward you: But I beseech you, that I may not be bold when I am present with that confidence, wherewith I think to be bold against some, which think of us as if we walked according to the flesh. For though we walk in the flesh, we do not war after the flesh: (For the weapons of our warfare are not carnal, but mighty through God to the pulling down of strong holds;) casting down imaginations, and every high thing that exalteth itself against the knowledge of God, and bringing into captivity every thought to the obedience of Christ.

The strongholds that Paul is talking about in this text are not devils and demons. The strongholds referred to are imaginations. In other words, thoughts, ideas and concepts. He's not talking about casting out devils; he's talking about casting down imaginations (thoughts, ideas and concepts) that are contrary to God's Word. These negative thoughts will try to convince you that you're just wasting your time and that there is no way that God can do this for you. If you don't cast these thoughts and imaginations down, then they will become strongholds.

That's right! A negative thought can become a stronghold. A negative idea can become a stronghold. A negative concept can become a stronghold. And believe me, it can have an effect on the outcome of your Prayer of Petition.

We limit God when our thoughts, ideas and concepts are not in agreement with His Word. A friend of mine recently preached in a church that had never heard about God's desire for them to prosper. When he showed them from the Word, the pastor of the church was in shock. His mouth just dropped opened. The church was in the middle of a building project and struggling with coming up with the finances, and my friend said, "You know, you can build this new building debt-free if you truly believe what the Word says."

No one in the church had heard of such a thing. Not only that, but they didn't even try to believe it. To them, this just wasn't possible. What happened? That thought, that religious mindset, had created a barrier, or a stronghold, which became a limitation. Their thought was: "We will never be able to build a building without going into debt for it." Well, dwell on that long enough and it creates a barrier. Unfortunately, you will live the rest of your life thinking that there is no way that you will ever acquire a thing in your life if you don't go into debt for it.

If you don't cast out negative imaginations, thoughts, ideas and concepts, they will limit God in your Prayer of Petition. Not only do you have to cast them out, but you also have to replace them with positive thoughts (there is no such thing as a vacant mind). There is no greater place to find positive thoughts than in the Word of God. The Bible says that all the promises of God are "yes" and "amen" in Him (see 2 Cor. 1:20).

You have to get in line with God's Word. You have to get in line with what He says is true. You have to pray the Prayer of Petition with your eyes fixed on the good report—on God coming through for you—and direct your attention away from the naysaying thoughts (from you or from others) that try to convince you otherwise.

Everything that God says you can be, you can be. Everything that God says you can have, you can have. Nothing—and I repeat, absolutely nothing—can stop you from experiencing what God says is yours, if you can see it in your mind and in your heart. Paul wrote that he was "persuaded that he [God] is able to keep that which I have committed unto him against that day" (2 Tim. 1:12).

Being persuaded is being in a place beyond doubt. When you pray the Prayer of Petition, you need to set your mind right. You need to fix your thoughts on God's ability to be your Source and provide all you need. You need to be like Paul and become a man or woman who believes that you can be and that you can have whatever God says in His Word.

Be persuaded that your healing will come. Be persuaded that your marriage can be restored. Be persuaded that your child will come to know the Lord. Be persuaded that your husband will start coming to church. Be persuaded that you can overcome that addiction. Be persuaded that you can live your life debt-free.

If you are ever going to experience the fullness of God, if you are ever going to experience the answer to your Prayer of Petition, if you are ever going to see God work in your life to turn seemingly impossible situations around, then you are going to have to rid yourself of negative thoughts and start believing that what God says is true.

You can shape for yourself a better future by reshaping your thoughts now. This is part of what Jeremiah wrote: "For I know the thoughts and the plans I have for you, says the Lord, thoughts and plans for welfare and peace and not for evil, to give you hope in your final outcome" (Jer. 29:11, *AMP*).

Notice how God's thoughts are connected to your future. Wouldn't it stand to reason that if you think the same thoughts as He thinks, then your future will match His plan? Think about it. Whatever God says is true in His Word is true in your Prayer of Petition. That's the whole point of this particular prayer. You are praying His will. You already know what He wants for your life. So start sowing good seed and good thoughts so you can see good results!

Get Addicted to the Word

The apostle John tells us, "Beloved, I wish above all things that thou mayest prosper and be in health, even as thy soul prospereth" (3 John 1:2). The phrase "even as" can be defined as "in direct proportion to." Here's what it says, if we read this verse using the latter definition: "Beloved, I wish above all things that thou mayest prosper and be in health, [in direct proportion to your soul prospering]."

The soul is made up of the mind, will and emotions. What is a prosperous soul? One in which the mind is renewed, the will is conformed to the will of God and the emotions are under the control of God's Word. A renewed mind is a mind that is selective about what it thinks. A renewed mind is a mind that casts down imaginations and every high thing that attempts to exalt itself against the knowledge of God. A renewed mind does not allow negative thoughts to hang around; it replaces them with what God says in His Word.

You can only renew your mind through constant fellowship in and with the Word of God. You will become what it says you can become. If you allow God's Word to create an image on the inside of you of the way God wants you to live or the way God sees your life, and you keep thinking about those things, and you continually meditate upon them, then nothing can keep them from coming to pass in your life.

If you see your Prayer of Petition coming to pass, then nothing can stop it from becoming a reality. But you must stay in the Word to build your faith and to keep your mind thinking on the right thoughts.

The Bible teaches us how important it is to regularly spend time in the Word. "This book of the law shall not depart out of thy mouth; but thou shalt meditate therein day and night, that thou mayest observe to do according to all that is written therein: for then thou shalt make thy way prosperous, and then thou shalt have good success" (Josh. 1:8).

Think the Word. Not just on Sunday. Not just at your small-group meeting. Not just during a revival. Not just 30 seconds before you go to bed. Meditate on God's Word all the time. Ponder it. Keep it in your mind. Keep it in your thoughts by day and by night. Obviously, if you are ever going to be this dedicated to the Word, then you're going to have to develop some discipline. Being this dedicated may not come naturally to you, and that's okay. Just keep at it! And then one day it will become your lifestyle.

Most Christians today don't like the word "discipline." "Discipline" comes from the word "disciple." What is a disciple? A disciple is a disciplined one. Too many of us think that a disciple is just anybody who claims to be a Christian. Let me tell you, there are a lot of undisciplined Christians. And consequently, they are not experiencing God's best for their lives.

Be so devoted to the Word that you get addicted to it. Get to the point in your spiritual life where you cannot get enough of the Word. When you pray the Prayer of Petition and stand on God's Word and allow it to saturate your soul, there is no way the devil—or anyone or anything else—can keep you from experiencing the answer to your prayer.

Here's one more thing. Not only do you need to meditate on the Word day and night, but you also need to act on it. "Do according to all that is written therein" (Josh. 1:8). It is not enough to simply mentally agree that the Bible is true. You must believe it and put it to work in your life. You have to act on it. You have to do what the Word says to do.

Treat God's Word the way it should be treated—as something very valuable and precious to you. If you've ever been sick and there was just nothing medical science could do, and it took the Word of God to bring about your healing, then you know how precious the Word is. If you were ever in a financial bind, and there was nowhere you could turn to get that financial need met, but the Word of God produced the result, then you know how precious the Word is. Don't ever lose that sense of value for the Word. It can do what nothing else can.

Study the Word. Meditate on it. Keep it before you at all times. Then your mind will become renewed. Your thought life will begin to line up with the Word of God. It will no longer be consumed by doubt, fear-ridden questions and negative thoughts. The peace of God will totally saturate your very being.

While peace is promised to you, I must warn you again—the kingdom of darkness will try to rise up against you when you pray your Prayer of Petition. At times, you will find yourself in the fight of your life. Here is where you make your stand and determine that you will persevere and refuse to be swayed by the negative voices that tell you God will never hear your prayer.

God said that He would. Settle that in your heart and mind once and for all, and never, ever doubt it again. Remember what is written in 1 Peter 3:12: "For the eyes of the Lord are over the righteous, and his ears are open unto their prayers."

CHAPTER 9

Be Prepared to Stand

M ost people in the Church today want to live a faith life that is easygoing and smooth sailing. They want a Christianity that's comfortable. They certainly don't want to engage in spiritual warfare. But true Christianity is a fight.

I Know It's Not Easy

The fact that life is not easy is something you know by now. You are reading this book because you need some things changed in your life. You may be going through some tough times. You might even be on the verge of giving up. Your attitude at this very moment might be, "Brother Jerry, I don't know if I can stand it anymore. I just want to quit." I want to encourage you. Don't quit. Don't give up.

Keep standing!

This is why Jesus said that we "ought always to pray and not . . . turn coward (faint, lose heart, and give up)" (Luke 18:1, *AMP*). He knew that you would be facing some impossible-looking situations. He also knew you would be tempted to give up. You might be thinking, *Brother Jerry, you don't know what I'm going through.* Well, you are right. I don't know exactly what you're going through, but by now, you should know that I have been through a few things of my own.

I have faced a number of impossible-looking situations in the 40-plus years since I began walking in faith, serving God and preaching the gospel. I can tell you this much—God has never let me down. There has not been one time when He has ever disappointed me. I'm not telling you that trusting God for the impossible is the easiest thing I've ever done in my life. It wasn't always easy. But I've learned that I need to know how to persevere. I need to know how to be determined. I need to know how to stand.

Paul endeavored to explain this in the book of Ephesians: "Finally, my brethren, be strong in the Lord, and in the power of his might. Put on the whole armour of God, that ye may be able to stand against the wiles of the devil. For we wrestle not against flesh and blood, but against principalities, against powers, against the rulers of the darkness of this world, against spiritual wickedness in high places" (Eph. 6:10-12).

These principalities, powers, rulers of darkness and wicked spirits we wrestle with are demonic forces that try to stop us from continuing to walk boldly in our faith. I know this might sound somewhat scary to you, but it's an important fact to understand if you want to live in total victory.

Sometimes when we read this Ephesians passage, we are tempted to quickly gloss over the text without really thinking about just how serious its message truly is. But it's real. We're talking about rulers of darkness! Strongholds! Wicked spirits in high places! This isn't a fairytale; it is kingdom truth.

Luke gave us a powerful example of wrestling in the spirit realm when he wrote about what Jesus went through when he prayed in the garden before His crucifixion. Jesus was in agony. He was praying intensely. His spirit was broken. He was in a fight that would literally determine the destiny of the human race.

This is how Jesus prayed: "Father, if thou be willing, remove this cup from me: nevertheless not my will, but thine, be done. And there appeared an angel unto him from heaven, strengthening him. And being in an agony he prayed more earnestly: and his sweat was as it were great drops of blood falling down to the ground" (Luke 22:42-44).

Notice how intent Jesus was in His prayer. He was so intent that His sweat came out as drops of blood. He had His whole heart in His prayer, and it showed. Why? He had to pray with such fervor because the forces of evil were hard at work trying to stop the greatest story of all from happening. They were trying to stop the death and resurrection of Jesus Christ! Friend, spiritual warfare, spiritual darkness, is real. Having to stand for your Prayer of Petition is a reality.

We Have the Victory

Spiritual warfare is not something we should be discouraged by. We have to remember that we are not helpless. God has given us the ability through His Word and by His Spirit to win this battle. When we pray the Prayer of Petition, we have to believe a few things. We have to believe that something can be done. We have to believe that we have authority to change things.

Of course, we can't do any of this in our own strength. Remember, Paul told us to "be strong in the Lord, and in the power of his might" (Eph. 6:10). We don't have any strength or might outside of God. We can't depend on ourselves or on the eloquent words we use in our prayer or on how smart we are. We have to depend on God showing up and working through us to make a difference in the spirit realm.

I want you to be encouraged. God has called us to pull Satan's kingdom down. Satan's high places are not off-limits to us. While the devil has spent years building up some of these fortresses, all it takes is the fervent prayer of a believer to pull them down. Imagine that! The devil has spent an enormous amount of time creating darkness all over the world.

There are families, communities, cities and countries all over the world that are controlled by the kingdom of darkness. But guess what? God can turn to one Christian in whom He lives and reigns and empower him to say, "Bring that kingdom down in the name of Jesus," and it must obey. Wow!

Do you know how aggravating that is to the devil? Do you know how frustrated he feels when he has spent 2,000 years building up his kingdom over a city and someone prays it down in an hour? Do you know how upset he gets when he invests his time and energy trying to destroy a particular family, and a praying husband tears it all down in a day? This is what the power of God can do through us. Now that deserves a big "Amen"!

You Just Have to Take a Stand

Here's the thing. You will not be able to tear down the powers of darkness unless you are prepared to stand. Remember the words of Paul in Ephesians 6. I want to review these verses with you again to guide you as you stand on your Prayer of Petition.

First, Paul states, "Wherefore take unto you the whole armour of God, that ye may be able to withstand in the evil day, and having done all, to stand" (v. 13). If you are going to pray the Prayer of Petition, you might as well get it in your thinking right now that perseverance is a part of the deal. You will be required to stand. You will be required to hang in there. You must not give up. You must determine that quit is not an option.

Wouldn't it be wonderful if everything happened instantly? Of course it would. Now, I know there are times when answers to our prayers come immediately. But those times are not always the norm.

So you just have to take a stand in your mind and your heart that you are willing to stand even if it takes forever.

I have had many instant results, but most of the time I've had to wait. When I pray, I'm always expecting results but I am also prepared to stand. I am prepared to persevere whether it's for a minute, an hour, a month, a year or even longer.

As soon as I pray the Prayer of Petition, the next thing on my mind is, *Okay, now it's time to stand.* The sooner you understand that you are going to have to persevere in your prayer, the better off you will be and the less you will struggle with discouragement. If you are confident that God will answer your prayer, then you don't really mind waiting for it. Who cares how long it takes, just as long as it comes to pass.

Paul also gave us some instruction on how we can stand. He said, "Stand therefore, having your loins girt about with truth, and having on the breastplate of righteousness" (v. 14). "Truth" in this verse applies to the Word of God. You can't stand if you don't hang on to what God says (your prayer is based on His Word, after all!). Too many people tell me, "Brother Jerry, I've done everything to stand, and it's not working. I feel worse. I don't know what I'm going to do." What happened? They've let their belt of truth fall to their ankles. You can't truly stand unless you are holding on to the truth. This is what enables you to persevere no matter how long it takes.

Paul also talked about the "breastplate of righteousness." This breastplate assures you that you have the right to expect results. It is your right standing with God. It is a confirmation that God has heard your prayers. It is a confidence that whatever you are praying for will come to pass. The manifestation will come because you and God are on good terms; you are bound by a covenant relationship.

Paul continued his instruction and told us to cover our feet with the gospel of peace (see v. 15). But then he said something that bears the most importance. I know this because he wrote the words "above all," which is another way of saying, "By all means, do not forget the next thing I'm about to say."

"Above all," Paul wrote, "taking the shield of faith, wherewith ye shall be able to quench all the fiery darts of the wicked. And take the helmet of salvation, and the sword of the Spirit, which is the word of God: Praying always with all prayer and supplication in the Spirit, and watching thereunto with all perseverance and supplication for all saints" (vv. 16-18).

He reminded us to arm ourselves with the shield of faith, the helmet of salvation and the sword of the Spirit (which is the Word of God). I want you to notice something. When you read this passage, you will notice a semicolon (in some translations, it's a colon) separating the words "God" and "praying." The original text written in the Greek did not have that punctuation mark in the sentence. That syntax was added at a later time at the discretion of the translators.

If we look at these verses without the semicolon, we read about "the sword of the Spirit, which is the word of God praying . . ." The Word of God can pray. Once again, how? Out of your mouth. The Word of God can pray, but it needs an instrument to do so. And that instrument is you! When you are praying your Prayer of Petition, meditate on these instructions in Ephesians 6. Use the text as an instruction in how to stand and persevere while you are waiting for God to fulfill His promise.

Know that you will need to stand. Know that you will need to persevere. And know that you can do these things by putting on the armor of God.

Find a Prayer Partner Who Knows How to Wrestle

Romans 15:30 tells us, "Now I beg you, brethren, through the Lord Jesus Christ, and through the love of the Spirit, that you strive together with me in prayers to God for me" (*NKJV*). Notice how specific Paul was. He wants us to strive together in our prayers. In researching this a little further, I found that the words "strive together" mean to contend or wrestle. Paul literally wrote to the church in Rome that he wanted them to spiritually wrestle together, as he was doing, through prayer.

Paul was telling these men and women, "I want you to be serious about this. I don't want to hear a dear-God-bless-Paul prayer. I want you to be intent in your prayers. I want you to be earnest in your prayers. I want you to wrestle in prayer along with me." The way I see it, Paul was trying to build up tag-team wrestlers.

I used to love watching wrestling programs on TV. I grew up on that stuff. As a matter of fact, I had an uncle who used to be a professional wrestler. I would go with him to some of his matches. I tell you, when I was young, seeing those matches live frightened the living daylights out of me! The wrestling stars were so big and muscular, and when they fought, it looked like they were killing each other (I didn't know it was mostly a show at the time). I would watch my uncle fight against another wrestler with all his might, sweat pouring down his face and veins popping out on his neck. His opponent looked just as menacing and determined to win. They looked like they were fighting for their lives.

Only minutes after the match, I would sit in the dressing room with my uncle, and then the guy that my uncle had looked as if he were going to kill in the ring would walk by. The two of them would laugh and joke around like old buddies, as if they had never even fought one another. I couldn't believe it. I would think to myself, *Why is my uncle talking to that man? He's a bad guy!*

Eventually my uncle broke the news to me. Professional wrestling was a form of entertainment. I was a little disappointed, but it didn't stop me from continuing to watch the matches, especially if my uncle was in the ring.

As a kid, I couldn't get enough of the tag-team wrestlers. The way they worked together to win was impressive. If you've ever watched such a match, you know what I mean. Picture this with me. Two tag teams are poised to fight in a huge arena. Fans fill the seats, shouting, jeering and clapping. The wrestlers wear mean facial expressions and their bodies bulge with muscles. Two of them get into the ring, and after the bell sounds, one starts beating on the other. The loser's partner stays in the corner on the ropes, cheering his teammate on. The crowd goes wild, hoping for the blood of the wrestler who looks pinned under his formidable opponent. Blow by blow, the poor guy is getting totally beat up . . . or so it seems. Suddenly, the duo in the ring switch off to their pumped-up partners and these two new guys jump into the ring, one ready for revenge, the other ready to finish the beating.

They go at it like wild dogs. They wrestle. They sweat. They grunt. They scream. They punch. They strike. They grab arms and legs and do whatever they can to try to take down their opponent. After a few more minutes of intense grappling, their tag-team partners take their place. Now it's back to the original wrestlers to fight each other while their teammates take advantage of the break to catch their breath and rest a bit. This goes on for a while, and each wrestler takes a turn battling the other.

That is what I picture when I read Paul's letter to the church in Rome, asking them to wrestle with him in prayer. He was saying he needed a prayer partner. He needed someone to partner with him in battling the opponent. He was saying he needed a buddy to step in and help him engage in this battle. Don't we all need a prayer partner like that? I know I do!

I remember one day sitting in my office thinking about an impossible-looking situation that I was facing at the time. That particular day, my accountant had brought me the financial statement for our ministry. To put it mildly, it did not look good. I took out my Bible and was preparing to pray about this mess. But instead of focusing on the Word of God, my eyes kept dodging over to the financial statement. I became more and more discouraged. I just couldn't keep myself from looking at those numbers.

As I continued to meditate on the bleak report, my secretary popped her head in my office and said, "Brother Copeland's on the phone. He wants to talk to you." I picked up my phone and greeted him with a big hello. I immediately noticed the enthusiasm in his voice when we started talking. I remember thinking, *Come on! He shouldn't be allowed to be so chipper when I'm in such a grim state of mind.*

He asked me, "So, Jerry, what are you doing right now?" I should have said, "I'm just sitting here worrying, Brother Copeland." But that's not something you want to say to Kenneth Copeland. Instead I told him, "Just trusting God, just trusting God."

His response took me by surprise. "Well, that's the reason I'm calling you. I had you on my heart this morning, Jerry. I've been praying for you."

That got me pretty excited.

"Here's what I'm going to do," he continued. "I'm going to do your praying for you today."

"What?"

"I'm going to pray for your needs today. I don't want you praying anymore for the rest of the day."

At first, I didn't understand. "What do you mean, you're going to pray for my needs and I'm not going to pray anymore? What are you saying?"

"Well, I can pray better than you."

Really? I thought to myself with a bit of sarcasm in my thought.

"What I mean, Jerry, is that I can pray over your needs without having your pressure." I'll never forget what he told me next. "Since I'm going to be praying, I want you to go play."

I wanted to tell Brother Copeland that his advice didn't make any sense. How could I go play when clearly I had to stay in my office and worry? Our financial dilemma was serious. Certainly it wouldn't get better if I ignored it and went to play. Besides, I didn't even know what he meant by playing! So I asked him.

My good friend paused for a moment and said, "Get in your car and go drive somewhere. Go to the park. Go to the gym. Ride your motorcycle. Just go and do something."

"And you're going to pray?" I asked him again, still a bit unclear. "While I go play?"

"You got it!"

Needless to say, I took Brother Copeland's advice. I hung up the phone, grabbed my car keys and told my secretary that I would be gone for a while. "Where are you going?" she asked.

A big smile came over my face. "I'm going to go play!"

She looked at me with a look of pity. I knew exactly what she was thinking. *Poor guy, bless his heart. He let the pressure get to him and he finally snapped.*

When I got in my car, I sat in the front seat with my hands gripping the steering wheel. I didn't have a clue where to go. So I just started driving. About five minutes into my excursion, I heard the devil whisper, "You're dumb. You've got a serious situation back at the office and here you are running around and goofing off. What's the matter with you? Who do you think you are? You had better get back in there."

"No!" I shouted. "Brother Copeland's praying. And I'm playing." I had a strong confidence. I knew my prayer partner was on the job. He was in the ring finishing up the match. He was fresh. He was strong. There was no pressure on him. He was helping me fight my battle. And thank God the breakthrough I needed came in just a matter of days.

And you know what? I've done the same thing for him at times. I know the kind of battles he goes through and I am more than willing to be his teammate just like he has been mine. I'm telling you, there is great power in having a faithful prayer partner.

It's good to have someone who can strive together with you . . . wrestle with you . . . contend with you . . . fight with you. It's even better if this person is your believing wife or husband. Your spouse is the best prayer partner you can have. If you're not married, then find a friend who has strong faith—someone you trust and who is willing to go to battle with you.

The main thing is, just don't give up before your Prayer of Petition comes to pass. It's not easy, but God will give you His strength, His power and His might to get you to the other side.

It's Not Over 'Til It's Over

When you offer God your Prayer of Petition and it seems that you have been standing for a long time (too long, indeed!), you need to remember there is nothing wrong with God. There is nothing wrong with the Holy Spirit. There is nothing wrong with the Word of God. Don't ever blame God when it looks as though nothing is working. The problem is not God; it's our lack of determination to stand.

I like what the apostle Paul said: "Now thanks be unto God, which always causeth us to triumph in Christ, and maketh manifest the savour of his knowledge by us in every place" (2 Cor. 2:14). I believe that triumph is God's best for our lives. In other words, it's never over until God says it's over. And God will never say it's over until you triumph. Yogi Berra, who played for the New York Yankees many years ago, is famous for saying, "It ain't over till it's over." God says, "It's never over until you triumph." So refuse to give up until you triumph.

The psalmist wrote, "My soul, wait only upon God and silently submit to Him; for my hope and expectation are from Him" (Ps. 62:5, *AMP*). What are your expectations right now? Did they come from God? If so, then don't ever give up on them.

When people around you are trying to convince you that your Prayer of Petition is nonsense or that what you are asking for will never come to pass . . .

When the devil whispers in your ear that God would never do this for you . . .

When you feel like you are on the verge of giving up . . .

When you can see no way out of your situation, and your confidence in God to supply your needs and grant your heart's desires is waning, . . .

Remember that your expectations come from God. Remember that He will see you through. Remember that He is your Source. Remember that God is in the process of causing you to triumph even when it looks as though it's all over.

Friend, are you desperate for your breakthrough? Are you desperate for your miracle? Are you desperate for God to change the impossible into the possible? If your answer is yes, then take your stand and refuse to give up. And don't ever forget that once you do, you can count on God to work behind the scenes in your behalf.

CHAPTER 10

The Prayer of Petition
for Prosperity

I know that the word "prosperity" has gotten a bad rap, especially in religious circles. Many of God's people have been deceived into believing that God wants them to be poor. Don't misunderstand me. When we are financially blessed, it doesn't mean we should spend all of our money financing our material wants and cravings. Our number one priority should be the kingdom of God.

I want to make it clear that God wants us to prosper (see Ps. 1:3; 3 John 2). He wants us to enjoy financial freedom (see Deut. 28:1-14). But once again, prosperity is about keeping our priorities right. Psalm 62:10 states that when our riches increase, we should not set our hearts on those riches or trust them as our source. We should keep our hearts set on the Lord, our only true Source, and on His Kingdom (see Matt. 6:33). Deuteronomy 8:18 states that the Lord gives us the power to create wealth so that He can establish His covenant and advance His Kingdom through us. Prosperity is not about having enough to fulfill all of our lusts. It's not about hoarding up things. It's about not being enslaved by lack so that we can do what God has called us to. Don't make the mistake of only associating prosperity with material things; associate prosperity with the freedom to do God's will.

The truth is, if you're in lack financially, it creates pressure on every area of your life. We pray to prosper so that we can do the work of God. We need to be blessed so that we can be a blessing. How can you help someone in need if your checkbook is in the negative? How can you help a missionary if you barely have enough money to make your mortgage payment this month? How can you give something to the widow and her three small children if your cash flow is in the negative? It's going to be pretty hard to meet the needs of others without financial freedom.

Are you in debt? Have you not made your car payment this month? Are you living from paycheck to paycheck? Have you depleted your savings? Now, think about the ways that God can move in your life and release you from this bondage. Maybe this could be the year you will pay off your car. Maybe this is the year you could get out of debt. Maybe this is the year you will sow a large financial seed into the new church building.

Here is the reality: It takes money just to exist on this planet. It takes money to feed and clothe your family. It takes money to do the things that God wants you to do in helping to further His kingdom.

That's why each of us needs to learn how to pray the Prayer of Petition for Prosperity. It's really no different from any other prayer of petition with the exception that you are specifically asking God for finances.

The same fundamentals that I've talked about in the previous chapters will reappear in this chapter as it relates to the promise of financial prosperity.

Biblical Model for Prayer of Petition for Prosperity

Psalm 118 is a wonderful text to look at as it specifically concerns prosperity. There is a lot of faith-building truth found in each of the verses that create a foundation for a Prayer of Petition for Prosperity. Let's review it here.

Oh, give thanks to the LORD, for He is good!
For His mercy endures forever.
Let Israel now say,

"His mercy endures forever."

Let the house of Aaron now say,

"His mercy endures forever."

Let those who fear the LORD now say,

"His mercy endures forever."

I called on the LORD in distress;

The LORD answered me and set me in a broad place.

The LORD is on my side;

I will not fear.

What can man do to me?

The LORD is for me among those who help me;

Therefore I shall see my desire on those who hate me.

It is better to trust in the LORD

Than to put confidence in man.

It is better to trust in the LORD

Than to put confidence in princes.

All nations surrounded me,

But in the name of the LORD I will destroy them.

They surrounded me,

Yes, they surrounded me;

But in the name of the LORD I will destroy them.

They surrounded me like bees;

They were quenched like a fire of thorns;

For in the name of the LORD I will destroy them.

You pushed me violently, that I might fall,

But the LORD helped me.

The LORD is my strength and song,

And He has become my salvation.

The voice of rejoicing and salvation
Is in the tents of the righteous;
The right hand of the LORD does valiantly.
The right hand of the LORD is exalted;
The right hand of the LORD does valiantly.
I shall not die, but live,
And declare the works of the LORD.
The LORD has chastened me severely,
But He has not given me over to death.
Open to me the gates of righteousness;
I will go through them,
And I will praise the LORD.
This is the gate of the LORD,
Through which the righteous shall enter.
I will praise You,
For You have answered me,
And have become my salvation.
The stone which the builders rejected
Has become the chief cornerstone.
This was the LORD's doing;
It is marvelous in our eyes.
This is the day the LORD has made;
We will rejoice and be glad in it.
Save now, I pray, O LORD;
O LORD, I pray, send now prosperity.
Blessed is he who comes in the name of the LORD!
We have blessed you from the house of the LORD.
God is the LORD,

And He has given us light;
Bind the sacrifice with cords to the horns of the altar.
You are my God, and I will praise You;
You are my God, I will exalt You.
Oh, give thanks to the LORD, for He is good!
For His mercy endures forever (*NKJV*).

I love the thankfulness with which the author wrote this psalm. The text launches with an attitude of gratitude. We cannot be reminded enough of this element in the Prayer of Petition. We need to be grateful. We need to thank God. We need to appreciate all He has done for us and all He will do for us.

In verse 5, the writer reminds God of previous petitions: "I called on the LORD in distress; The LORD answered me and set me in a broad place." He was giving testimony and saying something like, "I remember another time in my life when I was in great trouble and I called on the Lord; and He answered me and came through for me." Making a conscious effort to remember the last time you were in distress and God heard and delivered you goes a long way toward building your faith for the next impossible-looking situation.

I know I've talked about this before, but I believe I need to emphasize it again. When we find ourselves in an impossible-looking situation, we have the tendency to focus only on that problem. We only see the mountain in front of us. We don't look at the leveled plains behind us that were once mountains that God moved in our behalf. I believe this blindness, or short-term memory loss, is the work of the devil. He wants us only to set our minds on our immediate need, not our past victories.

I want you to do something. The next time you pray your Prayer of Petition and find yourself staring at that tall pile of bills on your desk, or you're holding a letter stating that you are now unemployed, or you're even looking at a foreclosure notice, ignore the temptation to pray: "Oh God, I don't know what I'm going to do. This is impossible. It's all over if You don't intervene."

Pray this instead: "Thank You, Lord. I just want to bless You. You are the Creator of the universe. You are the Source of my supply. You meet all of my needs. I bless You for my redemption. I thank You that I'm redeemed from the curse of poverty. I remember not too long ago when I didn't have money for food and gas and to pay the bills, and You miraculously saw me through. I also want to thank You for all of those other prayers that You've answered over the years. Lord, it would take me all day to praise You for all that You've done and for all that You are about to do."

Spend most of your prayer time in thanksgiving and then inject your petition in there somewhere. God doesn't need a lengthy monologue about what you need. He knows your needs; what He wants is your praise.

This is what the writer of Psalm 118 did. He spent the first 24 verses of this passage of Scripture praising God. He praised God for His mercy. He praised God for His protection. He praised God for His deliverance. He praised God for His strength. The psalmist invested much of his prayer time talking about who God is and what He has done. And this was all before he had even mentioned his petition. He spent a whole lot of time being grateful before he even considered asking God for a single thing.

There are a lot of folks out there who pray: "Dear God, my name is Jimmy. Gimme-gimmie-gimmie." "I need this. I want that." "Please do this. Please do that." Let's remember the greatness of God every time we stop and say a prayer for anything. Don't let anything come out of your mouth before you begin with thanksgiving.

In verse 25 we finally see the petition of the writer: "Save now, I pray, O LORD; O LORD, I pray, send now prosperity." I want you to notice how long this man's prayer time would have been if we eliminated everything but the actual request. One verse. That's it. No more than a few words. When it's time to make a Petition for Prosperity, you need to articulate what you are asking for. Petitions are specific requests. They are simple. They are to the point. And they are definite. Here are some examples.

"Dear Lord, I ask you to heal my finances."

"Dear Lord, I ask you to help me sell my house."

"Dear Lord, I ask you to help me buy that property for the new youth building."

"Dear Lord, I ask you to help me get that job."

The writer asked God for prosperity and then went back to thanking Him (see v. 26). He presented his petition and moved on to more important matters—continuing to praise God. This Petition for Prosperity has all the ingredients of the Prayer of Petition. It has the actual request (prosperity). It is seasoned with thanksgiving from beginning to end. And we also see the psalmist's humility in verses 8, 9, 18, 26 and 27. He never loses sight of the fact that God alone is his source for everything, and it's only in Him that he will find success (see Prov. 3:5-7).

God Wants You to Prosper

In his petition, the psalmist obviously believed it was the will of God that he prosper, or else he would not have been so confident about injecting that specific request into his prayer. In the same manner, you need to know it's the will of God that you prosper, or you won't have any confidence in your petition. You have to know deep down in your heart that He wants you to prosper. If you don't, then you'll never have any confidence that God will fulfill your petition.

I want to prove that this is God's desire for you through some passages of Scripture. I want to use His Word to speak to you so that you understand that His will is for you to prosper.

"Let them shout for joy, and be glad, that favour my righteous cause: yea, let them say continually, Let the LORD be magnified, which hath pleasure in the prosperity of his servant" (Ps. 35:27). This text offers a simple point—God gets pleasure out of you prospering. When I discovered this verse some years ago, I lifted both hands and said, "I promise I won't rob You of any more pleasure. I'm going to prosper." God delights in our success just as any good parent delights in the successes of their children. If you are a parent, don't you rejoice when your son or daughter is blessed?

I'm blessed each and every time one of my daughters or one of my grandchildren achieves success in any of their endeavors. Whether it's in sports, academics, their careers or their families, I rejoice over their every triumph, every win, every success. And God feels the same way about us. I like to picture my heavenly Father getting a kick out of seeing me winning in the game of life.

I remember how my father treated me when I was a little boy. I played Little League, and my dad came to every game, cheering me on with all his might. He got so excited when he saw me play, especially if I played well. When I would pitch a no-hitter game, he went ballistic. You would have thought he was the one throwing the ball! He walked around all week with a big ol' grin on his face, patting me on the back and telling everybody, "That's my boy." He was so proud that he would tell everyone he came in contact with how well I played. It was embarrassing, but I appreciated every word he said.

Obviously, I didn't win every game. As a matter of fact, I lost a number of games. That didn't make Dad love me any less. No, sir. He loved me whether I won or lost.

Don't think for one minute that God loves you any less if you don't prosper. He loves you regardless, but He gets His greatest joy when you do prosper and when you do succeed. I want you to get this truth deep into your heart. Here's a little spiritual exercise for you. You can pray this right now and start believing it from this moment forward.

Heavenly Father, as of this day, _____ [write in today's date], I refuse to rob You of any more pleasure. I refuse to rob You of any more joy. I want You to have great delight in me. Therefore, from this moment on, as one of Your children, I declare that I will prosper. It's Your will for my life, and I refuse to settle for anything less.

Let's take a look at some more Scripture:

Keep therefore the words of this covenant, and do them, that ye may prosper in all that ye do (Deut. 29:9).

This book of the law shall not depart out of thy mouth; but thou shalt meditate therein day and night, that thou mayest observe to do according to all that is written therein: for then thou shalt make thy way prosperous, and then thou shalt have good success (Josh. 1:8).

Pray for the peace of Jerusalem: they shall prosper that love thee (Ps. 122:6).

Beloved, I wish above all things that thou mayest prosper and be in health, even as thy soul prospereth (3 John 2).

God said it, and so it is settled. We have the authority of His Word that it is His will for us to prosper. Now we have to get it down in our spirit-man. We do that by reminding ourselves of His Word. Memorize these passages of Scripture. Meditate on them. Speak them out loud. Get them deep into your soul. When you pray the Petition for Prosperity, include them in your prayer. When you do, all you are doing is returning His Word back to Him.

When you speak the Word of God in prayer, you give evidence of your legal right to what you are asking for in prayer. In this case, it is for you to prosper—to get out of debt, to buy a bigger home for your growing family, to build that new church in your community, to sow some seed into a ministry.

Just the Facts, Ma'am

You already know that the Prayer of Petition deals with the known will of God. Your faith will only work on the level of, and cannot go beyond, your knowledge of His will. If you don't know what God's will is, your faith will not become strong. You can't shout enough or psych yourself out enough to try to make yourself believe in something that you don't know is the will of God or not. That's because you have no facts, and your faith only deals with facts. Jesus said that God's Word is truth (see John 17:17). It's factual. It's what we rely upon.

Here's what I mean as it concerns finances. Back in the day, when I traveled and ministered in convention centers around the country, our organization had to come up with a budget to finance the event. Today, my budget isn't that complicated. I don't have bands or singers or a lot of people going with me, but back then I did. When I say we had budgets, boy, we had *budgets!* You can't imagine the amount of money it takes to do a crusade. We had to pay for flights, hotels, food, convention centers, TV and radio advertisement. All these things add up, and fast.

Our budget was fixed, so at the end of every day, the finance co-ordinator and I would meet and discuss how we were doing. I hated this part. I hated even more when I wouldn't get specific details of how we were doing. When I'd ask, "Where are we on our budget?" I couldn't stand it when I got this kind of response, "Well, we're *about* so-much." *About?* I didn't want to hear about any *abouts.* My faith won't work on *abouts.* I wanted facts.

Now if I was given specific information like, "We are $6,000 short," for instance, I would have something to work with. I would have a target. My faith would have somewhere to aim. Now I could know what to continue to believe for.

Think about it. If they told me we needed *about* $6,000, but the actual figure was $6,417, what would happen? I would have the facts wrong and couldn't effectively pray the Petition for Prosperity. I would pray for $6,000 and come up $417 short.

You wouldn't go to a bank and tell the loan officer you needed about $5,000. Of course not! You would tell him exactly how much money you needed, right down to the last penny.

This reminds me of a story Brother Kenneth Hagin told. He has spoken hundreds of altar calls in life, but one in particular stood out in his mind. After he made the invitation to the church and a handful of folk gathered at the front of the sanctuary, Brother Hagin walked around and listened to the people as they started to pray. Every once in a while he would stop by someone and listen to what the person was saying. He was curious to see what they were asking of God.

There were many instances when he actually stopped someone in the middle of his or her prayer and asked, "What are you praying for, sister?" "What are you praying for, brother?" and was shocked to hear the reply, "Oh, I don't know, Brother Hagin, nothing in particular, I guess. I'm just praying." I love the way he responded, "Well, that's exactly what you are going to get then, nothing in particular."

Faith deals with facts. When faith does not have facts, it's like putting water in your gas tank. It won't run. It's not going to work. You might as well shut the thing down.

Be a Seed Planter

You can quote Scripture all day long, but there is another principle in prosperity that you have to apply in order to truly activate the Word of God. You have to plant something. Prosperity is described in the Bible as a harvest. It revolves around the law of sowing and reaping.

We read in Galatians, "Be not deceived; God is not mocked: for whatsoever a man soweth, that shall he also reap" (Gal. 6:7). Whatever you sow, you reap. Whatever you give, it will be given to you. Prosperity is not just something that happens. It comes as a result of something you do. It comes from sowing not just once, but continually and consistently.

I like to say that you have to be a seed planter (a sower). I'm not telling you to do something that I don't do in my own life. I'm constantly planting seeds. I tithe. I give to those in need. I help those who are less fortunate. I don't do these things so that I look good in front of others. I do it because God has blessed me. But not only that, I give because I know I will receive and that will enable me to be able to give even more. Love is the ultimate motivation for giving. The Bible says that because God loved the world He gave Jesus (see John 3:16). Because this same love has been placed in my heart (see Rom. 5:5), it is in my nature to give too.

God has given certain promises to seed planters that do not apply to anybody else. Here's what I mean. There are a lot of people going around confessing Philippians 4:19 ("My God shall supply all your need according to his riches in glory by Christ Jesus") who really have no right to confess it. Let me give you some background on that text.

Paul wrote those words to the people who had partnered with him in his ministry. They supported him financially and had invested in his ministry. Paul was talking about the principle of reaping because they were sowers and had sown into the work Paul was doing.

I know that tithing is not a popular subject to talk about. People get very sensitive when it comes to their money. But the fact of the matter is that tithing is a kingdom principle. There is no way around it. If you are a believer, if you profess the faith, if you expect God to bless you financially, you have to stop being stingy and start giving a portion of your money back to Him.

When you pray the Petition for Prosperity and, at the same time, you tithe and plant a seed to the poor or to those in need, you have more evidence to support your case. You have an advantage. I don't know about you, but I want every possible advantage there is when it concerns my Petition for Prosperity.

Giving or sowing your money into the Kingdom is not going to make God love you any more or any less than He already does or will, but it will show Him that you truly believe His Word and that you are a "doer" of it and not just a "hearer."

It also plays a part in fulfilling your covenant. If God says He will do x because you do y, then be sure you do whatever y is. Obedience is the door-opener to the miraculous.

I want you to write this verse down somewhere where you can see it. Put it on a Post-It or note card in your Bible, your checkbook or on your bathroom mirror.

Bring ye all the tithes into the storehouse, that there may be meat in mine house, and prove me now herewith, saith the LORD of hosts, if I will not open you the windows of heaven, and pour you out a blessing, that there shall not be room enough to receive it (Mal. 3:10).

Let me tell you about an example of this Scripture being used in a prayer of Petition for Prosperity and the results it received. Before my father-in-law, Olen Creech, (who now resides in heaven) retired, he had his own business building houses. I remember a particular time when work was slow and he was believing for more jobs. I can't remember what was going on at that time, but I think it was during a time of bad economy. Obviously, when you don't work, you don't make money. And even though he wasn't in debt or behind in bills or anything like that, he just wanted more work.

He visited with Brother Copeland and told him about his problem. My father-in-law wanted him to come into agreement with him that God would bless his business even if the economy was bad and there were no job opportunities in the construction business. I'll never forget what Brother Copeland told him: "Gather all your tithe check stubs and put them in a pile. Then show them to God as you pray and remind Him that you are a tither and that He promised to bless the tither."

Brother Copeland and my father-in-law read the promises concerning tithing in Malachi and then prayed. Olen said, "Father, based on the authority of Your Word and based on my obedience to do Your Word, I now call on You to fulfill Your promise on my behalf. Pour out blessings upon me and rebuke the devil who is trying to stop my business."

Wouldn't you know it, only a few days later, my father-in-law testified that he had so much work, he had to pick and choose the jobs he wanted. He had more than enough! That was some powerful advice Brother Copeland gave him.

Perhaps you need to look through your checkbook and pray this same prayer if your finances seem to be blocked. Remind God that you are a tither and a sower, and ask Him to honor His Word in your behalf.

You can do this on your own; you don't need me or Brother Copeland to do it with you. Just go to the Word and speak it out in your Petition and then expect God to bring it to pass. God is faithful, and He watches over His Word to perform it.

Be the Lender, Not the Borrower

I really believe that the next thing I am going to show you will break loose some roadblocks in your finances. So let me encourage you to read this very closely.

It's simple. If you have been blessed, then be a blessing. I believe in that fundamental principle so much that it's now a way of life to me. I live it every day. The Bible tells us that when we give to those in need, there is something in store for us as well.

Proverbs gives us some wise advice: "He that hath pity upon the poor lendeth unto the LORD; and that which he hath given will he pay him again" (Prov. 19:17). Did you know that when you give an offering to those who are less fortunate than you, you make a loan to God? It may sound crazy, but I didn't make that up. It's written right there in Proverbs. Let's look at another verse from the Old Testament: "The LORD shall open unto thee his good treasure, the heaven to give the rain unto thy land in his season, and to bless all the work of thine hand: and thou shalt lend unto many nations, and thou shalt not borrow" (Deut. 28:12).

Both of these verses talk about us becoming lenders. And in both cases, God says that He will bless us. He's saying that if you will do what He says, you will be so blessed that you won't have to borrow; you can be the lender. But that's not all. On top of that, if you give to the poor, then you are lending to God. Now think about this. Don't you think that God pays back His loans? You better believe it!

I want to give you a personal example. Years ago, I prayed a Petition for Prosperity for a very serious financial situation that my ministry had been battling for over a year. As I fellowshipped with God, He began to deal with me about how to pray regarding these circumstances. He reminded me of some things I had already learned from His Word and then opened up some new revelation to me. I started to write my petition and then presented it to Him.

I prayed, "God, the reason that I am unable to pay my bills is because I'm not seeing Your Word fulfilled. I have loaned You money and I'm not seeing it come back. You said You would repay me. So I'm standing on what You said, and I believe I receive in Jesus' name."

I hope you don't think this was crazy talk. All I was doing was approaching God on the authority of His Word. I was reminding Him of what is written in His Word. He's the One who made the promise that I was standing upon, so I felt I had every reason to expect Him to bring it to pass.

I went a step further and got out all my records to investigate exactly how much money I had given to the poor. I added up all the receipts and found out the total was in the thousands of dollars. I showed this figure to God and prayed, "All I'm asking, according to the facts and figures that I've laid out before You, is for You to honor what You promised in Your Word."

That was my petition. I didn't demand anything from God. I simply petitioned Him. I knew what His Word said and I also knew that He promised that it would never return unto Him void (see Isa. 55:11). Do you know what happened? He answered my prayer before midnight. That's right, I'm not exaggerating. It came to pass that very day.

I want to remind you of something the psalmist said in a passage we looked at earlier: "The Lord is on my side . . . the Lord taketh my part" (Ps. 118:6-7). This is covenant talk. He's our covenant partner. God actually told me this one day when I was praying. He said, "You are not putting enough of a demand on My Word. Even though I've said all of these things, it is you reminding Me of what I said that puts it in motion." Always remember this, we don't remind God of what He has said because He has forgotten it. We remind Him of what He has said because He told us to.

God's part of our prayer life is His Word. When we remind Him of His Word, we are demonstrating unto Him that we've taken the time to read it and we have also determined in our hearts that we are going to believe it. We're the ones who set things in motion. When God has promised us what He will do, then He waits for us to do our part so that He can then bring it to pass.

Let me show you what this meant in my prayer. As I was praying my Petition for Prosperity, the Lord asked me, "Have you done everything I commanded you to do?" I answered, "Yes, I have." He continued, "Have you made all the adjustments in your ministry that I commanded you to do?" I answered again, "Yes, I have." God asked, "Have you dealt with all the things that are not profitable?" I answered, "Yes, I have."

I told Him, "I can say with all honesty that I have done exactly what You have commanded me to do." He then said, "Then the only thing left is for me to do everything I said I would do." I said, "That's what I'm expecting because I know You are faithful."

Here's the deal. My financial situation was, as I previously stated, very serious. As a matter of fact, it was the worst financial attack I have ever experienced. However, I never stopped my giving. Things were tough in my organization, the biggest of which was my television ministry. I couldn't justify staying on TV and paying those astronomical costs with all the debt I had and, at the time, could no longer afford to pay. In the natural there was no way out.

But because of what I knew His Word said, and because I knew that I had acted on it, I had the legal right to expect Him to bring it to pass. And as I previously stated, He did. Only a short time later, my television ministry was restored and all the bills were paid. And I didn't even have to pay a dime for production or airtime costs! God spoke to the owners of the stations and instructed them to give us our air time for free. All I was required to do was promote their stations on my broadcasts. God does indeed move in mysterious ways!

God wants us to be free. God wants us to be liberated from debt and financial bondage. God wants us to be blessed and to be a blessing to others. We have a right to ask Him for prosperity. We have a right to present to Him a Petition for Prosperity based upon the authority of His Word. And we have the right to expect Him to move in our behalf.

Remember Your Source

Prosperity is God's best—even in a recession. It's not a matter of *if* it happens; it's a matter of *when* it happens. It's just a matter of time. Jeremiah 17:5-6 says, "Cursed is the man who trusts in mankind and makes flesh his strength, and whose heart turns away from the LORD. For he will be like a bush in the desert and will not see when prosperity comes, but will live in stony wastes in the wilderness" (*NASB*). Once again, not *if* it comes, but *when*.

I began this book by telling you that God is your Source. The foundation for the Prayer of Petition is to understand that only God can provide for all of your needs. All you need to do is trust in Him. He's bigger than any need you'll ever have. God is the One in whom you can always rely.

This verse in Jeremiah tells us that those who do not look to God as their Source will not see prosperity. They will wind up being like a bush in the wilderness, or as *THE MESSAGE* puts it, "like a tumbleweed on the prairie." The one who does not trust in God will be as unstable as his or her surroundings. In other words, if the economy is unstable, that person will be unstable.

Prosperity in the midst of turbulent times will come to those who believe and live by the truth that God—and God alone—is their Source. Prosperity in the midst of turbulent times will only come to those who believe God to be their King eternal, immortal, invisible, the only wise God (see 1 Tim. 1:17).

Determine today that you will not look to anything or anyone but God as your Source of supply. If you do not look to God as Source, then it's not likely that you will live a blessed life. I don't know about you, but I want to be blessed.

Don't Stop Learning

If you have had a hard time trusting God as your Source, I want to encourage you to keep reading the Word. That's how faith comes. Keep reading faith-inspired books. Become consumed with CDs and DVDs that have positive, faith-building messages on them. It does take time, and it means making the commitment to get into the Word every day of your life. If you will, then that absolute trust in God as your Source will come. And that truth will become a reality in your life.

We have to continually study and put into practice what God has said in His Word. When I first went to flight school many years ago, I was still spending most of my days traveling in the ministry. It was hard for me to interrupt my schedule and attend classes as much as I would have liked. I'd take one class and then travel and minister for a week. When I'd get back to school, I felt like I had to relearn whatever I was taught the previous week. It was very difficult to stay up with the program.

One day I found out I could go over to Love Field in Dallas and take a three-day accelerated course. The instructor squeezed in a lot of information in a small period of time. I was in class for 12 hours a day for three straight days. Plus I had homework each night. When I completed that course, I felt like my brain was on fire.

Although I passed the written exam and soaked up a lot of knowledge, it didn't make me an expert in flying airplanes. There was still much more to learn. Brother Copeland has been flying for more than 55 years, but he still takes flight safety courses. He is always learning, and that's what makes him a great pilot.

That's how God wants us to live—always learning. He wants us to grow in our faith. He wants His Word to dwell richly in our hearts so that we can be assured that when we're in need, we know what He has said and we can then expect Him to bring it to pass.

Don't ever stop learning. In Philippians 3, Paul talked about how his greatest desire was to know God. At the time he wrote that letter, most theologians agree that his relationship with Christ had continued somewhere between 10 and 20 years. So even though Paul had been walking with God for a long time, he knew there was still so much to learn.

Keep studying the Word. Keep believing. Keep standing. Keep persevering. Whether you have done this for 7 days or 70 years, God wants you to keep on growing up in Him and building your faith. If you truly want to live a blessed life and if you truly want results from the Prayer of Petition, then keep trusting God. He is never going to let you down.

I want to share one more story with you to encourage you to never stop trusting God. Keep believing that He is the One who causes you to prosper even when the rest of the world does not believe it. On a ministry trip to Tanzania recently, I was reading an article in one of the popular newspapers. It talked about how charitable organizations like the Red Cross and the United Way were suffering because contributions were at an all-time low. This was true, of course, because the economy was not doing well.

After reading this article, I said out loud, "This will not affect me." I forgot I was reading this on a commercial airplane. (Usually, I'm in our ministry airplane.) The guy sitting next to me looked at me as if I was nuts. He said, "What do you mean?" I read the article to him and stated that I was a minister with a charitable organization, but I didn't believe this would affect me. Obviously, he didn't understand, but that didn't really matter. I understood, and that's what counts.

After I had been in Tanzania for a few days and ministering to others, doing outreaches, helping out orphanages and feeding the poor, I was overwhelmed by the Spirit of God. I felt so blessed that my staff and I could be a blessing to these wonderful people. The opportunity we had to minister to and feed and clothe them was a privilege. I was grateful for our partners and friends that had enabled us to do all of this.

Later on that trip, my daughter Terri received an email from our office in the U.S. She informed me that while we were there, back home we had just received the biggest contribution our organization had received for the entire year. We immediately started praising God. Once again, He was proving that even in a bad economy, He was our Source.

This is what happens when you believe God to make the impossible happen. He is our Source. He is our provider. He will never let us down. If you dare to trust in Him, He will bring blessings into your life that you would never have imagined.

Sample Prayer of Petition for Finances

I want to make something clear. When you pray the Prayer of Petition for Prosperity, you are not asking for things that are not His will. Make sure that you ask in line with His Word. Don't just say things that sound spiritual or religious. Say what His Word says. Also, be sure to pray for finances that will help further the kingdom of God. As I've previously said, God wants you blessed so that you can be a blessing.

You might be on the verge of losing your house. You might be on the verge of losing your church. You might be on the verge of losing all that you have saved over the years. You have the right to pray for financial blessing.

If you are in a place today where you need God to step in and help your financial situation, here is a prayer for you.

Be it known this day, _____, _____ (A.M./P.M.), that I receive a heavenly grant in the amount of $_____. Father, in the name of Jesus, I come boldly to the throne of grace, and present Your Word.

According to John 16:23, Jesus said, "I assure you, most solemnly I tell you, that My Father will grant you whatever you ask in My Name" (AMP).

Jesus, You said in Mark 11:24, "Whatever you ask for in prayer, believe (trust and be confident) that it is granted you, and you will [get it]" (AMP).

Your Word states in Luke 6:38, "Give, and it shall be given unto you; good measure, pressed down, and shaken together, and running over, shall men give unto your bosom." In accordance with Your Word, I give and I sow seed, in order to set this spiritual law to work in my behalf.

Because I am "a cheerful (joyous, 'prompt to do it') giver [whose heart is in his giving]," You make "all grace (every favor and earthly blessing) come to me in abundance, so that I am always and under all circumstances and whatever the need self-sufficient [possessing enough to require no aid or support and furnished in abundance for every good work and charitable donation]" (2 Cor. 9:7-8, AMP, with personal paraphrase).

According to Matthew 18:18, I bind Satan and all his forces, and I render them helpless and unable to operate against me. They will not hinder my grant.

According to Hebrews 1:13-14, I loose the ministering spirits, and I charge them to go forth and cause my grant to come into my hands.

I have applied for this grant for the following:

Agreement (when appropriate):

Jesus, You said in Matthew 18:19, "Again I say unto you, that if two of you shall agree on earth as touching any thing that they shall ask, it shall be done for them of my Father which is in heaven." Therefore, _____ and I set ourselves in agreement, and we believe we receive now, and we praise You for it.

_____   _____

(Signature)   (Date)

CHAPTER 11

A General Look at Prayer

W hile this book has focused on providing you with an in-depth view and application of the Prayer of Petition, I want to conclude this teaching by talking about prayer in general. In my years of study, I've found there are different types of prayer addressed in God's Word. I want to show you how you can apply them in your life.

Why Pray?

Prayer is the responsibility of every believer. Some people think that having a mature prayer life is reserved for the older believer or for just the women in the church. The truth is that every Christian has the privilege, the right, and the responsibility to develop a strong prayer life. We should not turn to prayer only when trouble comes or during special meetings. We should maintain an open dialogue with our heavenly Father throughout the day, every day.

In its most basic form, prayer is simply talking with God. Communication is the foundation for any growing relationship, including our relationship with Him. I encourage you to make a habit of talking with God everywhere you go and in everything you do—in your car, on your lunch break, as soon as you wake up in the morning, the moment your head hits the pillow at night.

Prayer is not a religious duty. Prayer is a privilege of the believer. Through prayer we can share our heart with the Lord as He shares His with us. It is a dialogue, a conversation with our heavenly Father.

Jesus is our example of how we should pray. Prayer was a lifestyle that He modeled for us during His ministry on earth. "Then Jesus told his disciples a parable to show them that they should always pray and not give up" (Luke 18:1, *NIV*). "But Jesus often withdrew to lonely places and prayed" (Luke 5:16, *NIV*).

He prayed among the hypocrites. He prayed in crowds. He prayed on a hillside crowded with people. He prayed alone at night. If prayer was important to Jesus, and we are supposed to live our lives exemplifying Him, prayer should be equally as important to us.

So many Christians ask God what His will is for their lives. Without a doubt, it is God's will for you to pray: "Be joyful always; pray continually; give thanks in all circumstances, for this is God's will for you in Christ Jesus" (1 Thess. 5:16-18, *NIV*). If you pray continually, then God can direct you into other areas of His will for you as well.

God can actually be hindered from moving on our behalf when there is a lack of prayer in our life. Colossians 4:2-3 says, "Devote yourselves to prayer, being watchful and thankful. And pray for us, too, that God may open a door for our message, so that we may proclaim the mystery of Christ, for which I am in chains" (*NIV*). We learn from this verse that through prayer, God can open doors of opportunity in our life. In the same vein, He can also close doors. I like what John Wesley said: "It seems God is limited by our prayer life—that He can do nothing for humanity unless someone asks Him."

The Bible is full of great men and women of faith who lived a lifestyle of prayer:

Abraham (see Gen. 20:17)
Moses (see Num. 11:2; 21:7)
Hannah (see 1 Sam. 2:1)
Samuel (see 1 Sam. 8:6)

Elisha (see 2 Kings 4:33)

Isaiah (see Isa. 38:12)

Jeremiah (Jer. 32:16)

Daniel (see Dan. 6:10)

Jonah (see Jon. 2:1)

And, of course, we can't forget about the New Testament examples like Paul and Peter.

Types of Prayer

When you have a need that you want to pray for, the most effective way to communicate with God regarding it is to know what kind of prayer will most benefit you in your particular situation. That's what Paul meant in Ephesians 6:18 when he told us to pray always, with all kinds of prayer. The seven different types of prayer or praying that I have discovered in the Bible include:

1. The prayer of petition and supplication (see Eph. 6:18)
2. The prayer of intercession (see Rom. 8:26-27)
3. The prayer of praise and thanksgiving (see Luke 24:52-53; also found in many of the psalms)
4. The prayer of agreement (see Matt. 18:18-20)
5. The prayer of faith (see Matt. 21:22)
6. The prayer of dedication and consecration (see Matt. 6:10; Acts 9:6)
7. Praying in the Spirit (see 1 Cor. 14:15)

When you pray, you will notice that many times you operate within more than just one type of prayer. For instance, in the

Prayer of Petition, we have discussed the need for praise and thanksgiving, praying in faith and how the prayer of agreement can be applied.

In this closing chapter, I want to concentrate on the subjects of the prayer of intercession, the prayer of agreement and praying in the Spirit. My purpose for this is simply because, as I have previously mentioned, the quickest way to have your needs met is to get involved in the needs of others.

The prayer of intercession has nothing to do with praying for yourself. It literally means "to get the ear of God in behalf of someone else." Interceding for others while you're waiting for your own Prayer of Petition to be fulfilled is a great way to demonstrate to God that you truly believe that He has not only heard you but that He is in the process of bringing your prayer to pass.

The prayer of agreement also has the same effect while you're waiting for your prayer to be answered. Learn to stand in agreement with someone else for their needs to be met. By doing so, you are also applying another very powerful spiritual law: "Do to others what you would have them do to you" (Matt. 7:12, NIV). Don't you enjoy having others stand in faith with you? The Bible clearly teaches us that there is power in agreement (see Matt. 18:19).

Finally, the reason I want to discuss praying in the spirit is because we don't always know how to pray the perfect will of God in our own understanding and particularly when we're praying for others. By praying in the Spirit, or in other tongues, as the Bible refers to it, we can be assured that the Holy Spirit knows the perfect will of God and He will enable us to pray as He prays through us. We'll talk about this more in the conclusion of this chapter.

The Name Above All Names

The most important key to a successful prayer life is praying to our Father God in Jesus' name. In fact, that's how you should go to the Father in prayer every time you pray. Jesus said in John 14:6, "I am the way and the truth and the life. No one comes to the Father except through me" (*NIV*). He went on to teach His disciples some principles on how to pray.

> In that day you will no longer ask me anything. I tell you the truth, my Father will give you whatever you ask *in my name*. Until now you have not asked for anything *in my name*. Ask and you will receive, and your joy will be complete. Though I have been speaking figuratively, a time is coming when I will no longer use this kind of language but will tell you plainly about my Father. In that day you will ask *in my name*. I am not saying that I will ask the Father on your behalf. No, the Father himself loves you because you have loved me and have believed that I came from God (John 16:23-27, *NIV*, emphasis added).

Please know this: saying "in Jesus' name" at the end of a prayer shouldn't be done just because it's the religious thing to do. There must be a true meaning behind the words you speak—true faith in the power in that name and, most importantly, you must have a personal relationship with Jesus in order to use His name in power.

The name of Jesus is very powerful. Even the demonic realm recognizes this truth. "Then some of the itinerant Jewish exorcists took it upon themselves to call the name of the Lord Jesus over those who had evil spirits, saying, 'We exorcise you by the Jesus whom Paul preaches.' Also there were seven sons of Sceva, a Jewish chief priest, who did so. And the evil spirit answered and said, 'Jesus I know, and Paul I know; but who are you?' " (Acts 19:13-15, *NKJV*).

There is nothing greater than His name. The name of Jesus is above all things. "Therefore God elevated him to the highest place and gave him the name that is above every name, that at the name of Jesus every knee should bow, in heaven and on earth and under the earth" (Phil. 2:9-10, *NIV*). Whatever situation you are dealing with—debt, sickness, distress, confusion, rebellion—the name of Jesus is more powerful. When you go to the Father in Jesus' name, you are going to Him in the authority and the power of Jesus.

I can remember times while growing up when my mom would ask me to go and tell my sister to do something, whether it was to clean up the kitchen or to take out the trash. Whenever I told her to do it, however, she sometimes ignored me. Eventually, I'd say, "Mom wants you to do this." Suddenly, my sister became alert and attentive and did whatever it was Mom had told me to tell her to do.

What was the difference? Why did she ignore me but then pay attention when I said "Mom"? She knew when I came to her on behalf of Mom, I came to her with Mom's authority and power. It's the same way when we pray. As we pray in Jesus' name, we come in the power and the authority of Jesus Himself.

The Prayer of Intercession

In simple terms, intercessory prayer is prayer for others, or praying on the behalf of others. Our greatest example of an intercessor is Jesus, who "ever liveth to make intercession" for us (Heb. 7:25).

When He left the earth, He sent us the Holy Spirit to help us intercede for others. Romans 8:26-27 says, "Likewise the Spirit also helpeth our infirmities: for we know not what we should pray for as we ought: but the Spirit itself maketh intercession for us with groanings which cannot be uttered. And he that searcheth the hearts knoweth what is the mind of the Spirit, because he maketh intercession for the saints according to the will of God." In the original Greek, the word "helpeth" means to "take hold together with." The Holy Spirit takes hold with us to help us pray.

God has given us spiritual legal ground to stand on for our intercession for others. Remember, the Word is always our foundation, and it says, "But he that is joined unto the Lord is one spirit" (1 Cor. 6:17). Since Jesus is an intercessor and we are one spirit with Him, we are also intercessors. He is the Head, we are His Body; and we are one with Him in carrying out His work in the earth.

Intercessory prayer is a beautiful thing. We can move mountains on behalf of others and facilitate a move of God in their lives. We can pray for our friends, our family, our loved ones. We can pray that God will meet whatever need they may have. We can stand in the gap for others and help see them through their trials and tribulations.

The Bible gives us many examples of intercessors.

- Abraham prayed for Sodom and Gomorrah (see Gen. 18).
- Moses prayed for Israel (see Exod. 32:32; Num. 14:13-19; Deut. 9:26).
- Moses prayed for Miriam (see Num. 12:13).
- Job prayed for his friends (see Job 42:10).
- Samuel prayed for Israel (see 1 Sam. 7:5).

- David prayed for Israel (see 1 Chron. 21:17).
- Hezekiah prayed for the people (see 2 Chron. 30:18-20).
- Elisha prayed for Israel (see 1 Kings 17:1; Jas. 5:17-18).
- Jesus prayed for Peter (see Luke 22:32).
- Paul prayed for the Galatians (see Gal. 4:19).

We can make intercession for many different things. You can pray for your son or daughter to get saved (see 1 Tim. 2:4). You can pray for your spouse's life to be changed in some way (see Gal. 4:19). You can pray for God's intervention, whether in your marriage, your job situation or your emotional or mental healing (see Dan. 10:12). You can pray for boldness in someone's ministry (see Eph. 6:19-20). You can pray against sin (see 2 Cor. 12:21). You can pray for deliverance from an addiction or stronghold (see 2 Thess. 3:1-3). You can pray for your beloved country (see 1 Tim. 2:1-4).

When you intercede and pray as one with God, you will see His transforming power at work in circumstances, individuals and nations.

The Prayer of Agreement

The prayer of agreement is also a very powerful prayer tool. "Again I say to you that if two of you agree on earth concerning anything that they ask, it will be done for them by My Father in heaven" (Matt. 18:19, *NKJV*).

There are times when the Holy Spirit will direct you to agree in prayer with another believer concerning a need or an issue. We saw this in chapter 4 with friends of mine who wanted to buy a house, as well as in chapter 10, when Brother Copeland prayed with my father-in-law over his job situation. Don't ask just anyone to agree with you. You need to be sure that the person agreeing with you for what you are asking of God is strong and stable in his or her faith.

One of the reasons this type of prayer can be so effective is because there is power in unity. The Bible shows us in Genesis 11:6 that when people came together, united for a single purpose, nothing could stop them. That's the type of power available in the prayer of agreement.

The prayer of agreement means that two or more people have come together in harmony of faith (in the Word) and are standing together until their prayer is answered. It becomes the heartfelt prayer of each person involved. God promises that He will bring to pass whatever they have agreed upon.

Praying in the Spirit

This powerful gift is a "cannot fail" weapon in your prayer arsenal. It is praying out of your spirit with Spirit-given utterances in a tongue that is unknown to you (see Rom. 8:26).

First Corinthians 14:15 teaches us that we can pray both with our understanding (our mind) and out of our spirit: "What is the conclusion then? I will pray with the spirit, and I will also pray with the understanding. I will sing with the spirit, and I will also sing with the understanding" (*NKJV*). There are several great reasons why you need to pray in the Spirit:

- It builds you up spiritually (see 1 Cor. 14:4; Jude 1:20).
- It enables you to pray the will of God when you don't know what to pray or how to pray for a particular situation (see Rom. 8:26-27).
- It refreshes and brings rest (see Isa. 28:11-12).

Perhaps the most important reason is that through it we can obtain wisdom from God about how to pray even as we're praying. "For he that speaketh in an unknown tongue speaketh not unto men, but unto God: for no man understandeth him; howbeit *in the spirit* he speaketh mysteries" (1 Cor. 14:2, emphasis added).

First Corinthians 2:6-7 explains this even further: "However, we speak wisdom among those who are mature, yet not the wisdom of this age, nor of the rulers of this age, who are coming to nothing. But we speak the wisdom of God in a mystery [or in the Spirit], the hidden wisdom which God ordained before the ages for our glory" (*NKJV*). This "hidden wisdom" translates into God's perfect will. It may not be known to your understanding when you first began to pray, but the Holy Spirit through you and in you is helping you to pray it to the Father.

As you pray in the Spirit, you may not have immediate understanding of what you are saying; but when you pray in faith in the Spirit, the wisdom will come. You can understand the mysteries of God through this means in several different ways:

- You "hear" a still, small voice inside your spirit.
- The Holy Spirit may direct you to a Scripture or bring revelation of a Scripture as you read the Word.
- You may be reminded of something someone else shared with you that now makes better sense to you and seems to line up with what you have been praying about.
- You may remember a message by your pastor, small-group leader or devotional leader that contains the answer you were looking for.

Whatever revelation you receive, here is the important thing to remember: It must line up with James 3:17: "But the wisdom that is from above is first pure, then peaceable, gentle, and easy to be entreated, full of mercy and good fruits, without partiality, and without hypocrisy." The Word "pure" implies that it must agree with God's Word. God will never tell you something that does not line up with His Word.

Have You Forgiven Lately?

One last thing I want to remind you of is something we often forget or simply don't think about. One of the reasons many Christians do not see the results available to them through prayer is because they harbor unforgiveness in their hearts. If you do not forgive others, your prayers will be hindered.

Jesus was very clear on this issue: "And when you stand praying, if you hold anything against anyone, forgive him, so that your Father in heaven may forgive you your sins" (Mark 11:25, NIV). Don't allow grudges or past hurts to keep you from receiving the answers to your prayers. It might not be easy to forgive those who have betrayed you or hurt you, but the results are worth it. You can never move forward and receive what God wants for you if you refuse to forgive someone who has offended you.

There was a time many years ago when I needed a breakthrough in my ministry, and though I was praying and believing, nothing seemed to change. I prayed, but my miracle never came. Something seemed off-kilter and I knew it wasn't God, so it had to be me.

One day when I was talking with the Lord about this situation, He reminded me of a certain minister that I had a problem with.

This minister had done some things that I did not agree with, and I had developed a grudge toward him. I wasn't going around talking bad about him, but whenever I heard his name brought up in conversation, this negative feeling would rise up on the inside of me. It was like a twisting knot in my stomach. God spoke to me simply and clearly: "Forgive this man."

I immediately told my wife what had happened. "Carolyn, the Lord showed me that I need to forgive this minister. This unforgiveness is blocking my prayers from being answered." A few days after I forgave this man and released those negative feelings I was carrying around with me, I was at a conference and saw him there. I walked right up to this man, gave him a hug, and asked him to forgive me.

The experience completely changed me from the inside out. I was free in my heart and very shortly after that experience, I received my breakthrough. God is so faithful!

There is so much more to learn about this act called prayer. Someone once said, "The best school of prayer is praying." I agree; don't ever stop praying.

Pray always. Pray in your car. Pray while you take a walk. Pray as you clean your house. Pray on the job. Pray with your spouse. Pray with your kids. Pray with your friends. Pray over the things you are struggling with. Pray for situations where you need God's intervention. Pray over whatever is troubling you.

And above all else, pray in faith. Trust God and believe. Believe that God can do all things. Believe that He can make the seemingly impossible, possible. Believe that God can take your situation and turn it around in your favor. Because, friend, He can!

Study Guide Questions

CHAPTER I

God Is Your Source

We have been called to pray. As believers, our faith walk is encouraged, strengthened and uplifted through prayer. But first and foremost, we need to understand the One to whom we are praying. The One who is our everything. The One who is our Source.

1. Read Psalm 62:5-6. How do you relate to the psalmist who writes how God alone is his rock, savior and hope? Do you have that same kind of relationship with God?

2. Reflect honestly for a few minutes about your life. Think about where you place your trust. Do you trust in your spouse, your boss, your manager, your agent, your parents, your teachers or your counselor more than you trust in God?

3. Think of a situation where you had put your trust in someone or something other than God and found yourself disappointed. What made you trust God less than this person or thing? What was it about that person or thing that made you trust them more than God?

4. When you hear the words "trust God," how does that make you feel? Empowered? Unsure? Confident? Skeptical? Excited? Afraid? Reflect on your feelings and write down what might lie at the root of those feelings. For example, if you feel unsure about trusting in God, perhaps you don't completely believe that God can provide for all of your needs because your parents neglected you in some areas.

5. Do you consider yourself self-sufficient? Do you have a hard time trusting God as your Source because you believe you can control and take care of all kinds of circumstances or obstacles in your life? Read Proverbs 3:5-6. How can you better live out the truth found in this Scripture?

6. Perhaps fully trusting in God comes naturally and easy for you. Why do you think that is? Reflect on a situation or two that seemed impossible in the natural, but God supernaturally provided for your need or answered your prayer. How did that experience strengthen your faith? Do you believe it can happen again?

7. Read Matthew 6:25-34. What strikes you about this passage? Do you find yourself worrying about day-to-day details or your future? How does reading this passage help you take one day at a time and rest in God's care?

8. Read Ephesians 3:20, Proverbs 3:5-6 and 2 Corinthians 9:8 and include the words "my Source" every time there is mention of God.

9. What are the top three things that you find yourself worrying about? (For example, finances, your marriage, your children.) What are some ways that you can intentionally lessen your worry and increase your trust in God?

10. How has reading this chapter and learning how God is your Source changed or invigorated your prayer life?

CHAPTER 2
The Prayer of Petition

The Prayer of Petition is a specific prayer supported by evidence and facts based on the known will of God through His Word. I have found that the Prayer of Petition brings about the quickest results in what seems to be impossible situations. It is not a prayer prayed in haste or one that is prayed without a deep understanding of what you are asking for and what God says is possible in your situation. It is a specific prayer for a specific need.

1. How important do you think prayer is in the life of a believer?

2. Read the following excerpt from chapter 2:

> I am going to make you a promise. The Prayer of Petition will enhance and energize your prayer life. It will change you. It will make things happen. It will bring you to places you never could have otherwise gone. You know as well as I do that if there is anything the Church needs right now it's an energized prayer life that brings results. The fact is, there are some things that are happening in the spirit world right now that will never manifest in the natural if they are not birthed in prayer. Are you ready for it?

What did your prayer life look like when you first read this book? Was it powerful? Was it continual? Was it sporadic? Was it weak? How has it changed since then?

3. How do you feel about incorporating the Prayer of Petition into your regular prayer life? How do you see it working in conjunction with your regular prayer life?

4. What are some impossible-looking situations that you are struggling with right now? Do you believe the Prayer of Petition can make a difference in those difficult circumstances?

5. What is the difference between the Prayer of Petition and other kinds of prayers?

6. See the basic definitions of the word "petition" on page 36. How have you found those descriptions helpful in understanding and crafting your Prayer of Petition? Does it help you take it more seriously? Does it help you understand the formality of it?

7. Read the story again about my first Prayer of Petition on pages 38-40. How did that story encourage you? How did it build up your faith?

8. Read Psalm 20:5-9. How can you parallel that biblical passage with your Prayer of Petition? Is it a faith-building reminder?

9. Have you talked to any of your friends, family or colleagues about the Prayer of Petition? Are they encouraging or discouraging you in the process? If they are not supportive in your belief, how can you keep your eyes on God instead of allowing others to sway your faith?

10. What are some areas in your life where you plan on constructing a Prayer of Petition?

CHAPTER 3
Supplication

Supplication is another component of the Prayer of Petition. Though it is an inclusive part of this unique type of prayer, it has a special meaning. When Paul told us to pray "always with all prayer and supplication" (Eph. 6:18), he had a distinctive purpose in using the word "supplication."

1. Explain the difference between petition and supplication. How do they work together in the Prayer of Petition?

2. Review the definition of the word "supplication":

   • An urgent petition
   • To make an earnest request
   • An entreaty

   What are some earnest requests you have in your heart that you need to present to God?

3. How does the Prayer of Petition and Supplication keep you from being spiritually lazy or living your faith on the sidelines of life?

4. Think of some examples when you have prayed earnestly for something. How did your prayer differ from a God-bless-me-today-thank-You-for-everything-and-amen kind of prayer?

5. Read the story in Acts 12:1-19 about Peter's unjust imprisonment. How do you view this situation as impossible? If you look

at his situation in the natural, do you think there was a way out of his situation? Does this story remind you of something happening in your own life where you see no way out?

6. Read 1 Thessalonians 5:17. How do you interpret the words "without ceasing"? How is your prayer life affected by the accurate meaning of this verse?

7. When was the last time you prayed for something or someone where you were intensely stretched out in that particular prayer and your whole heart was in it? What did that prayer look like?

8. How do you think God feels when we pray with our whole heart? Read James 5:16. What is the difference between a prayer that is prayed half-awake, without conviction, and half-hearted versus a prayer that is earnest, to the point and that may even be unable to be articulated because of inner groanings?

CHAPTER 4
Prepare Before You Present

The Prayer of Petition is like a spiritual legal document. It is not mumbo-jumbo, and it requires diligent preparation. It's about actively seeking to know God's will for your life in your specific situation. It's about gathering the necessary information to construct a prayer that gives you the confidence of getting results.

1. What is a particular situation for which you are planning on praying the Prayer of Petition?

2. Outside of reading this book, have you ever spent time studying the Bible to see what God says about your particular impossible-looking situation? What do you already know God's Word says about your situation?

3. Do you believe the Bible contains everything you need to figure out what His will is for your life? Why or why not?

4. As I mention in the chapter, the first thing you need to know in preparing your Prayer of Petition is that you are asking for something in line with God's will. Let's go on a fact-finding mission. What does God have to say about your situation? For instance, if you are praying for healing, research what is written in the Bible about God's will in that area. If your situation concerns finances, research what the Bible says about financial prosperity.

5. Read 1 Corinthians 2:11. The Holy Spirit is your guide to help you understand the Word of God as it relates to His will and

your particular situation. How has the Holy Spirit spoken to you in the past to help you in your faith walk? Has He guided you in your prayer life? How can you ask the Spirit of God to become a part of helping you create your Prayer of Petition?

6. Who or what is the final authority in your life? Why? Have you experienced instances when you purposely chose to rely on God's Word rather than what a doctor, teacher or a well-meaning friend had to say? What to you is the determining factor that gives God's Word the right to have the "final say"?

7. Read the story in this chapter about my sick father. Imagine that you were in my shoes. What would you have done in that situation? Would you have relied solely on the medical diagnosis and prayed for something other than immediate healing? Or do you think you would have trusted in God to have the final say over the negative report?

8. Do you pray the Word of God in your prayers? Have you spent time memorizing Scripture to build up your faith? Write down some Bible verses that you can use in your Prayer of Petition.

At this point, I recommend that you buy a notebook designated only for Prayers of Petition. Write down all the prayers you pray over the course of the next few years, and keep it close to you so that any time you need some encouragement or faith-building, you can pull it out and read how God has answered your prayers. Also, take some time to construct a

Prayer of Petition based on what you have learned in this chapter. Write it down. Don't forget to write down the passages of Scripture that speak about your situation.

CHAPTER 5
Thanksgiving

Everyone likes to feel appreciated. Having an attitude of gratitude is not only necessary to have deep and meaningful relationships with others, but it is an important part of the faith walk. Thanksgiving is a particularly vital part of the Prayer of Petition. God favors people who have an attitude of gratitude. You cannot begin and end this prayer without thanking the One who makes it all possible. In fact, it's one of the first things you should do when you pray.

1. When is the last time someone thanked you for doing something or just for being who you are? How did it make you feel?

2. Why do you think thanksgiving is such a big deal to God? Why is it an important thing to do in your prayer life?

3. Why do you think there are many people in the world today who are ungrateful for God's blessings? Why do you think it is so hard for people to give God praise? Do you sense a spirit of entitlement among God's people? Do you think some of them believe they "deserve" God's blessings and therefore do not have to be grateful for them?

4. What are three things you have never thanked God for that you might take for granted (for example, air conditioning, a roof over your head, family and friends who love you)?

5. Read this excerpt:

> The children of Israel had a bad habit of coming to God with a spirit of despair. This happened all the

time, even though God provided for them time and time again. What was their problem? They were ungrateful. When God delivered them out of Egypt and they went about their journey toward the Promised Land, they constantly murmured and complained about one thing or another.

They were quick to forget about the miracle of God leading them out of the land of slavery. They were quick to forget about the miracle of God parting the Red Sea so they could pass through to freedom. They were quick to forget about the miracle of God supplying them with manna from heaven every day.

What do you think about the fickle attitude of the Israelites? Can you relate to how they repeatedly vacillated from thanking God to complaining about their circumstances? Was there a time in your life when you did something similar? Write about it.

6. What are three prayers that God has answered in your life or three times when He has provided for you and seen you through?

7. Do you have a covenant with God? What does that mean to you? Do you feel divinely connected to Him in your prayers? How does that give you a confidence in praying the Prayer of Petition?

8. A. W. Tozer once said, "Gratitude is an offering precious in the sight of God; and it is one that the poorest of us can make and be not poorer but richer for having made it." How has an attitude of thanksgiving to God made your faith walk richer?

9. Usually, when we are grateful for God's provision in our life or even grateful because we believe He will provide, we are moved to sow into His kingdom. How has this principle been true in your life?

10. In what ways can you cultivate the habit of thanksgiving?

CHAPTER 6
Stop Worrying

Many of us have a tendency to worry. Worry is contrary to the Word, and it can stop God's blessings from flowing into our lives. One of the biggest temptations you will have after you construct and start praying your petition is that you will find yourself tempted to worry about all kinds of different things. Regardless of what worry plagues your soul, there are ways to stop it from affecting your Prayer of Petition.

1. Read this excerpt:

> I love the last line Jesus said: "O ye of little faith." I want you to know that God responds to faith, and wherever He finds it, He is drawn to it. Second Chronicles 16:9 tells us that "the eyes of the LORD run to and fro throughout the whole earth, to shew himself strong in the behalf of them whose heart is perfect." One of the meanings for the word "perfect" in this passage is a heart that has faith. God's eyes scan the earth looking for someone who believes.

   If God's eyes passed over your heart right now, what would He find? Would He find a person in desperate need of faith or a person who is strong in faith?

2. How does worry affect you in your day-to-day life? Your prayer life? When life seems relatively carefree? When trials and tribulations come your way?

3. Have you found yourself worrying since you started to pray the Prayer of Petition? What kinds of thoughts are you having?

4. Read this excerpt:

> Here is what's going to happen if you don't take control of that thought. If it gets in and stays in your mind, it's going to eventually drop down into your heart and then come out of your mouth. Before you know it, you will start talking that once-harmless thought. And when you start talking about it, you are going to—as I call it—block your blessing with your own words. God wants to prove Himself to you as your Source. He wants to show you that He has unlimited power; but if you are saying things that are contrary to His Word, then you will block Him from performing His Word.

When worry enters your mind, what happens to your thought life and your emotions? Are you able to control your thoughts and not allow your emotions to run wild? Do you think you could benefit from doing a better job at this?

5. Worry has the power to choke God's Word from manifesting in your life. Does this statement inspire you to stop worrying?

6. What is your immediate reaction when worrisome thoughts come your way?

7. Read 2 Corinthians 10:5. In what ways can you take your thoughts of worry and fear captive and surrender them to God?

8. Has any member of your family or a friend misinterpreted your lack of worry and your confidence in God as arrogance or pride? How did it make you feel? How did you respond in that situation?

9. How does it make your spirit feel to know that you are always in God's face? Does it take away some of the pressure you may be feeling? Does it provide you some comfort?

10. How can you relinquish your worry and pray for someone else? Is there a person right now that needs your prayers?

CHAPTER 7
More than Confident

When you pray the will of God, you can have confidence that the end result in the situation you are praying for will be favorable. Confidence comes when you ask God for something you know is in line with the Word of God.

1. Read 1 John 5:14-15. How does this passage of Scripture affect your Prayer of Petition?

2. Do you believe you have confidence in your prayer life? Why or why not? Write down an example.

3. Compare your faith walk today to what it was like a week, a month, a year or even a decade ago. Have you seen an increase of confidence in God over the years? Why or why not?

4. Read Psalm 37:4. What do you think about God supplying not only the things that you need in this life, but of giving you the desires of your heart? Are you comfortable with that or does it make you feel uneasy?

5. What are some things that you desire (e.g., a spouse, a new job, a child) for which you can create a Prayer of Petition?

6. Read Psalm 28:1-9. What are some phrases or sentences in this passage that stand out to you? How does it increase your confidence that God will answer your Prayer of Petition?

7. What has been your experience with doubt in your faith walk? Do you have a hard time trusting God? Why or why not? Do you rarely, occasionally or frequently have moments where you doubt God's provision or the fact that He does hear your Prayer of Petition?

8. Read this excerpt:

> When we doubt God's willingness, we doubt His love for us. The Bible says that God is love, so if we doubt His love, then we doubt the validity of His Word. My friend, I assure you, God's Word is true.

   Is this text something to which you can relate? Do you find it easy to believe that God can do great things yet you struggle in believing that God wants to do great things in your life?

9. What are some of your own favorite confidence-building Scriptures? Write these below.

10. How deep is your confidence in God to fulfill your Prayer of Petition? How can you further deepen that belief?

CHAPTER 8
Make Room for Peace

1. Read Philippians 4:6-7. How have you experienced God's peace covering you in times of great anxiety? How have you experienced God's peace in the midst of praying the Prayer of Petition?

2. How can you make God's peace a reality in your life?

3. Read the following excerpt:

> The greatest battles you will ever fight are in your mind. You can actually destroy the power of your prayer simply by what you think about. You must not allow your mind to run wild and think whatever it wants to think. You have the ability to keep it under control and allow the Word of God to dominate your thought life.

   What is on your mind right now?

4. When you pray your Prayer of Petition, do you find yourself having more negative thoughts or positive thoughts?

5. Can you think of instances in your life when you have sown negative thoughts and reaped the same? What about positive thoughts?

6. How do you combat the negative thoughts that come into your mind? Do you give them a chance to stick around and get sown?

7. What strategies can you put into place to saturate your mind with good seed—positive thoughts?

8. Read the following excerpt:

> Scripture teaches us to "look not at the things which are seen, but at the things which are not seen: for the things which are seen are temporal; but the things which are not seen are eternal" (2 Cor. 4:18). The word "temporal" means temporary. I love the definition the Lord gave me way back in the early 1970s. He said "temporal" means "subject to change."
>
> If you can see it, then your situation is subject to change. If you believe God's Word more than what your situation is telling you, then your situation is subject to change. If you pray the Prayer of Petition in faith and keep thinking right thoughts, then your seemingly impossible situation is subject to change.

How does this "subject to change" truth encourage you in your particular Prayer of Petition?

9. Are there people in your life—loved ones, coworkers, family or friends—who speak nothing but negative things? Do they influence you to turn your thinking into negative seed? What can you do to avoid contact with those people or ignore their destructive thinking?

10. What are some negative seeds that have become strongholds in your life? Take time to pray that God will break those strongholds and help you get in line with the Word of God.

CHAPTER 9

Be Prepared to Stand

You have read this book because you need some things changed in your life. You are probably going through some tough times. You might even be on the verge of giving up. Your attitude at this very moment might be, "Brother Jerry, I don't know if I can stand it anymore. I just want to quit." I want to encourage you. Don't quit. Don't give up. Keep standing!

1. Are you tempted today to give up? Have you been praying the Prayer of Petition for what you feel is too long? Has something happened to discourage you as you continue to believe God for what you are asking Him to bring about?

2. Think about a time in your past when you have faced impossible situations and have seen the hand of God move in your life. How can you use that experience to keep yourself standing?

3. Read Luke 22:42-44. Notice the fervency with which Jesus prayed. Can you find some comfort knowing that the Son of God, the incarnate God, was tempted to give up and give in? How can His experience in the Garden of Gethsemane before He was crucified strengthen you during the "waiting period" of your Prayer of Petition?

4. Read Ephesians 6:10-20. Meditate on the power we have through God to pull down strongholds. What are some ways that you can use the armor of God that Paul talks about to help keep you standing?

5. What has been your experience with answers to prayer? Do you tend to have to wait to get your prayers answered? Have you ever experienced immediate deliverance from God? Do you typically find yourself getting impatient or discouraged by the waiting process?

6. Do you have a prayer partner? If not, look around at your family and friends. Who would you want to commit to as a prayer partner? Talk to that person and see if he or she would be willing to partner with you.

7. Read the following excerpt:

> When you offer God your Prayer of Petition and it seems that you have been standing for a long time (too long, indeed!), you need to remember there is nothing wrong with God. There is nothing wrong with the Holy Spirit. There is nothing wrong with the Word of God. Don't ever blame God when it looks as though nothing is working. The problem is not God; it's our lack of determination to stand.
>
> Standing on your Prayer of Petition can be painful and difficult. Are you mad at God because you feel that you are waiting too long for your Prayer of Petition to get answered?

8. Read Psalm 62:5. How does this verse encourage you to keep standing until your Prayer of Petition is manifested? How does this encourage you to keep on trusting God?

9. Read James 5:10-11 in *THE MESSAGE*. This passage talks about how Job developed "staying power" through his trials and stood faithful until God triumphed over his circumstances. How can you develop your staying power?

10. For how long are you willing to stand?

CHAPTER 10

The Prayer of Petition
for Prosperity

1. Read the following excerpt:

   I want to make it clear that God wants us to prosper
   (see Ps. 1:3; 3 John 2). He wants us to enjoy financial
   freedom (see Deut. 28:1-14). But once again, prosperity is about keeping our priorities right. Psalm
   62:10 states that when our riches increase, we should
   not set our hearts on those riches or trust them as our
   source. We should keep our hearts set on the Lord,
   our only true Source, and on His Kingdom (see Matt.
   6:33). Deuteronomy 8:18 states that the Lord gives us
   the power to create wealth so that He can establish
   His covenant and advance His Kingdom through us.
   Prosperity is not about having enough to fulfill all of
   our lusts. It's not about hoarding up things. It's about
   not being enslaved by lack so that we can do what
   God has called us to. Don't make the mistake of only
   associating prosperity with material things; associate
   prosperity with the freedom to do God's will.

   How do you define financial prosperity?

2. Read Deuteronomy 28:1-14, Psalm 1:3 and Psalm 62:10. Do you
   believe God wants to prosper you? If so, in what ways? If not,
   why not?

3. How do you reconcile the true message of prosperity with the negative ways some have tainted this message?

4. Read the following excerpt:

> Are you in debt? Have you not made your car payment this month? Are you living from paycheck to paycheck? Have you depleted your savings? Now, think about the ways that God can move in your life and release you from this bondage. Maybe this could be the year you will pay off your car. Maybe this is the year you could get out of debt. Maybe this is the year you will sow a large financial seed into the new church building.

    Read Psalm 118. How much time do you spend thanking God versus asking Him for stuff?

5. If you are going through financial trouble right now, what are some ways that God has seen you through in this area in the past? How can you use those instances to keep believing?

6. Is there a particular area in your finances in which you need deliverance? Spend time constructing a Prayer of Petition for this need.

7. Read the following excerpt:

> Whatever you sow, you reap. Whatever you give, it will be given to you. Prosperity is not just something that

happens. It comes as a result of something you do. It comes from sowing not just once, but continually and consistently. I like to say you have to be a seed planter (a sower). I'm not telling you to do something that I don't do in my own life. I'm constantly planting seeds. I tithe. I give to those in need. I help those who are less fortunate. I don't do these things so that I look good in front of others. I do it because God has blessed me. But not only that, I give because I know I will receive and that will enable me to be able to give even more. Love is the ultimate motivation for giving. The Bible says that because God loved the world He gave Jesus (see John 3:16). Because this same love has been placed in my heart (see Rom. 5:5), it is in my nature to give too.

Are you a seed planter? Why or why not? If you are, in what ways do you sow into God's kingdom?

8. Have you been the recipient of divine intervention in the area of finances? Has someone provided for you at the very moment you needed it most? Share your experience.

9. Who is the source of your finances? Of your paycheck? Of your business? Of your credit card? Of your inheritance? Is it God? Why?

Further Resources

For additional products, including books, audios and videos,
visit the Jerry Savelle Ministries Int'l. website at

WWW.JERRYSAVELLE.ORG

- Daily Devotionals
- On-Demand TV Programs
- Product Specials
- MP3 Product Downloads
- Magazine Downloads
- Travel Itinerary
- And Much More...

JERRY SAVELLE
BIBLE SCHOOL

Three convenient ways to study at home:

ONLINE   CD-ROM   MAIL

To get started in this life-changing program
or for enrollment information, visit
school.jerrysavelle.org
or call 817-297-3155

LET THE CHAMPION IN YOU ARISE!

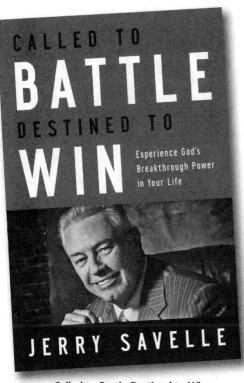

Called to Battle Destined to Win
Jerry Savelle
ISBN 978.08307.48051
ISBN 08307.48059

When tough times come, what do you do? Complain? Throw in the towel? Head home? If you are like most people, you give up. But God wants you to stay in the battle and prevail over whatever difficulties you are facing. God has chosen you to fight this battle, and He has given you a destiny to experience His breakthrough power. What's more, He will provide everything you need to pursue, overtake and recover what has been lost. Jerry Savelle has been in the battle and emerged to tell about it. Through enthralling stories, solid teaching and inspired motivation, he will show you how to persevere when situations are tough and stand on the Word of God until victory is achieved. The pain, disappointments or failures in your past cannot overcome God's purposes for your life when you trust His promise that He will always show up when you refuse to back down. So let the hand of God work in and through you to say no to giving up and yes to becoming a champion!